P9-DVO-860

CALGARY PUBLIC LIBRARY

OCT    2017

# NATIONAL GEOGRAPHIC KiDS

# QUIZ WHIZ 6

## 1,000 SUPER FUN MIND-BENDING TOTALLY AWESOME TRIVIA QUESTIONS

NATIONAL GEOGRAPHIC
WASHINGTON, D.C.

# Table of CONTENTS

# INTRODUCTION

## Are you ready to flex your brain muscles?

*Quiz Whiz 6* will strengthen your synapses, bulk up your brain cells, and give your gray matter a workout. Our quiz masters have spent months scouring libraries, mining the Internet, and interviewing experts to verify these facts that will beef up your brain.

Do you know where the rainiest place on Earth is? Who's the programmer behind the Minecraft games? Why did Malala Yousafzai win the Nobel Peace Prize? These pages contain more than 1,000 trivia questions about animals, geography, nature, history, science, pop culture, math, and amazing adventures. Each question will test your general knowledge of everything from the *Transformers* films to the Periodic Table of Elements to find out what you already know— and what you don't—as you sleuth out the correct answers.

Each page displays a different type of quiz game. Can you tell the truth from tall tales? "True or False?" quizzes have 30 statements about one topic. Use your awesome sense of direction to locate everything from famous archaeological digs to national parks on the "Map Mania!" pages. Can you pick the correct answer out of a pool of four tempting choices? Multiple-choice questions throughout the book cover movie and TV celebrities, ancient cultures, cuddly animals, great adventures, fantastic foods, wacky inventions, and bizarre sports. Each chapter ends with a "Game Show," where you'll find special photo questions and an extra challenging "Ultimate Brain Buster." Do you have what it takes to score 100 percent?

If you're a solo act, you can quiz yourself. But if you're a team player, challenge family and friends to a *Quiz Whiz* competition. The answers to all the questions are at the end of the book. As you add up your scores for each chapter, read the hints and tips to help you find out more. If your noggin starts to feel numb after a while, you can always revisit the book a few months later and see how your scores have improved. (You know they will—practice makes perfect!)

Whether you're up for a light workout or a mental marathon, these trivia questions will limber up your lobes. Even if you don't know all of the answers, you'll be learning lots of new fun facts. With all this extra exercise, you'll be proud of your bulked-up brain as you cross the finish line.

# In the WILD

AFRICAN ELEPHANTS AND GIRAFFES IN EAST AFRICA

# DYNAMITE DOLPHINS!

**1** **True or false?**
Dolphins live only in saltwater oceans.

**2** **What is a dolphin's tail called?**
a. bobbin      c. flipper
b. fluffy      d. fluke

**3** **How high can a bottlenose dolphin jump?**
a. just 3 feet (1 m)
b. about 6.5 feet (2 m)
c. up to 16 feet (4.9 m)
d. more than 20 feet (6 m)

**4** **Some dolphins use sea sponges as tools. What do they use them for?**
a. to build sand castles
b. to protect themselves while hunting
c. to attack other dolphins
d. to clean their homes

**5** **Which region of the world could you visit to see a common dolphin in the wild?**
a. the coast of Alaska
b. Mediterranean Sea
c. Iceland
d. the Great Lakes

**6** **True or false?**
Bottlenose dolphins use names for one another when they communicate.

**7** How can a dolphin manage to think about each breath it takes while sleeping?

a. Half of its brain sleeps at a time.
b. It builds an air bubble around its blowhole.
c. It sleeps on land.
d. A dolphin never sleeps.

**8** What do dolphins drink?

a. ocean water
b. seaweed juice
c. Coca-Cola
d. freshwater, from their food

**9** True or false?

"Dolphin" and "porpoise" are different names for the same animal.

**10** What happens when a dolphin uses echolocation?

a. A radio antenna comes out of its head.
b. It shoots bubbles at prey.
c. It makes clicking sounds.
d. It blows its nose.

**11** What happens if a dolphin loses one of its teeth?

a. A new one grows in.
b. Echolocation is impossible.
c. It replaces it with coral.
d. A permanent hole is left in its smile.

**12** How fast can a dolphin zip through the water?

a. 1 mile (1.6 km) an hour
b. 5 miles (8 km) an hour
c. 18 miles (29 km) an hour
d. 62 miles (100 km) an hour

**13** Which trick can a dolphin learn to perform?

a. jump through a hoop
b. balance a ball on its nose
c. swim backward
d. all of the above

**14** True or false?

Baby dolphins hatch from eggs.

BOTTLENOSE DOLPHINS LEAP HIGH OUT OF WATER.

CHECK YOUR ANSWERS ON PAGES 158–159.

# Bird WATCH

1. **What is the name of this stunning bird from the Central American tropical rain forest?**
   - a. watermelon bird
   - b. good-looking chick
   - c. resplendent quetzal
   - d. Zeus

2. **Like the baseball team, male Baltimore orioles have _____ coloring.**
   - a. blue and gray
   - b. bright orange and black
   - c. yellow
   - d. green and purple

TURKEY VULTURE

3. **What does a turkey vulture do to defend itself?**
   - a. uses wing spikes to prick predators
   - b. throws up smelly vomit
   - c. shoots poison feathers
   - d. burrows into the ground

4. **True or false?** In most bird species, the male is more colorful than the female.

5. **True or false?** Baby hornbills and their mother live inside a tree for about four months.

HORNBILL

6. **Which fruit is also the name of a New Zealand bird?**
   - a. papaya
   - b. banana
   - c. mango
   - d. kiwi

**7** Where does the toucan live?

a. Asia
b. Africa
c. South America
d. Europe

TOUCAN

**8** In which habitat would you find the greatest variety of bird species living together?

a. a pine forest
b. the suburbs
c. a city
d. the tropical rain forest

**9** Which bird, flying from Antarctica to Greenland, holds the record for the longest migration of any animal?

a. arctic tern      c. sparrow
b. seagull          d. grouse

CLIFF SWALLOW

**10** True or false? Human fighter pilots reach their top speeds faster than cliff swallows can.

**11** Birds of paradise of Papua New Guinea have uniquely shaped feathers that they use to _____.

a. attract mates
b. regulate their body temperature
c. help them fly
d. all of the above

**12** Which of these birds can't fly?

a. condor        c. cassowary
b. falcon        d. pelican

CHECK YOUR ANSWERS ON PAGES 158–159.

13

# CREEPY CREATURES

**1** On the Indonesian island of **Komodo**, what large animal do Komodo dragons hunt?

a. blue whale
b. water buffalo
c. polar bear
d. hippopotamus

**2** What does a **flying fox** eat?

a. spiders
b. fruit and flowers
c. blood
d. fish

**3** What marking does a **female** black widow spider have on her body?

a. blue star
b. purple stripe
c. red hourglass
d. skull and crossbones

**4** True or false? The Tasmanian devil has curved horns on its **head.**

**5** How is a **ghost** shrimp like a ghost?

a. It has a see-through body.
b. It says "boo."
c. It lives in graveyards.
d. It walks through walls.

**6** Which of these is a **real** creature?

a. cave troll
b. goblin shark
c. griffin hawk
d. zombie pig

KOMODO DRAGONS ON AN INDONESIAN ISLAND BEACH

**7** In what country are black cats traditionally considered **lucky?**

a. United States     c. Spain
b. Scotland     d. Japan

**8** **Scientists** found a fish in **Myanmar** with bone spikes for fangs and called it _____.

a. a dragon fish     c. a Dracula fish
b. a skeletor     d. an ogre face

**9** True or false? The vampire squid hunts and **kills** human divers.

**10** A crab with long, hairy arms is named **after** the _____.

a. Pegasus     c. Sphinx
b. satyr     d. yeti

**11** If a goliath bird-eating **tarantula** bit you, you would probably _____.

a. feel nothing
b. experience pain and nausea
c. go blind
d. die

**12** Where would you have to **travel** to find a devil frog?

a. below the ice of Antarctica
b. back in time to the Cretaceous period
c. inside a Hawaiian volcano
d. the moon

**13** True or false? The basilisk lizard can run on top of **water**.

**14** What does the **hagfish** do to get away from predators?

a. shoots slime at them     c. swims extremely fast
b. emits high-frequency noises     d. stabs them with its horns

CHECK YOUR ANSWERS ON PAGES 158–159.

# ANIMAL Acrobats

FLYING SQUIRREL

**1** What does a flying squirrel use its tail for?
**a.** to hang from branches
**b.** to scare predators
**c.** to steer and brake
**d.** to dig for nuts

**2** Frogs' legs work like which of the following?
**a.** spring
**b.** lever
**c.** pulley
**d.** rubber band

EUROPEAN TREE FROG

**3** Which bird flies upside down and backward, or hovers in place?
**a.** hummingbird
**b.** penguin
**c.** flamingo
**d.** ostrich

**4** Which insect can jump the highest?
**a.** ant
**b.** froghopper
**c.** flea
**d.** ladybug

**5** What part of a cheetah's body allows it to run faster than any other land animal?
**a.** muscles
**b.** skeleton
**c.** legs
**d.** all of the above

SPIDER MONKEY

**6** Spider monkeys have a prehensile tail, meaning they can _____ with their tail.
**a.** shoot venom
**b.** grab branches
**c.** write poetry
**d.** play basketball

16

**7** Sea lions perform acrobatic moves in the water to escape from _____ .
**a.** sharks          **c.** penguins
**b.** alligators      **d.** stingrays

**8** **True or false?** Polar bears can stand and walk on their hind legs.

**9** Which is the fastest fish in the ocean?
**a.** great white shark
**b.** tuna
**c.** sailfish
**d.** minnow

POLAR BEAR

**10** Which animal uses its tail like an extra leg when moving around?
**a.** chimpanzee      **c.** tree sloth
**b.** jackrabbit      **d.** kangaroo

**11** **True or false?** An elephant has more muscles in its trunk than you have in your entire body.

**12** **True or false?** The acrobat ant has eight legs instead of six.

**13** What is the name of this fast and agile African antelope?
**a.** subaru
**b.** ibex
**c.** impala
**d.** reindeer

ELEPHANT

ANTELOPE

# TRUE or FALSE?
# It's Classified!

1. DOLPHINS AND WHALES ARE FISH.

2. ALL LIVING THINGS ARE CLASSIFIED AS EITHER ANIMALS OR PLANTS.

3. "BINOMIAL," MEANING TWO-PART NAME, IS THE SYSTEM SCIENTISTS USE TO CLASSIFY LIVING THINGS.

4. LEONARDO DA VINCI DEVELOPED A SYSTEM SCIENTISTS USE TO CLASSIFY LIVING THINGS.

5. THE WORD "ARACHNID" COMES FROM THE GREEK WORD FOR "SPIDER."

6. THE PLATYPUS IS THE ONLY MAMMAL THAT LAYS EGGS.

7. THE CLOSEST LIVING RELATIVE OF *TYRANNOSAURUS REX* IS A BIRD.

8. HUMANS ARE ANIMALS.

9. HORSES AND RHINOCEROSES HAVE JUST ONE TOE ON EACH FOOT.

10. ALL LIVING THINGS USE DEOXYRIBONUCLEIC ACID (DNA) TO MAKE MORE OF THEMSELVES.

11. ALL MONKEYS ARE PRIMATES, BUT NOT ALL PRIMATES ARE MONKEYS.

12. HALF OF ALL LIVING VERTEBRATE SPECIES (ANIMALS WITH BACKBONES) ARE RAY-FINNED FISHES.

13. HUMANS, HAWKS, AND SALAMANDERS ARE ALL IN THE SAME PHYLUM.

14. THE WORD "AMPHIBIAN" MEANS "SLIMY CREATURE" IN LATIN.

15. BIRDS ARE MOST CLOSELY RELATED TO REPTILES.

**16** SOME FISH CAN LIVE ON LAND.

**17** THE SMALLEST PRIMATE IS ABOUT THE SIZE OF A HOUSE CAT.

**18** ALL MARSUPIALS COME FROM AUSTRALIA.

**19** THERE ARE NO ANIMALS WITH FIVE ARMS.

**20** BUTTERFLIES AND LOBSTERS ARE BOTH ARTHROPODS.

**21** MAMMALS ARE ANIMALS THAT PRODUCE MILK FOR THEIR BABIES.

**22** ALL BIRDS HAVE WINGS.

**23** BATS ARE A TYPE OF RODENT; THEY ARE MOST CLOSELY RELATED TO MICE.

**24** WHALES ARE MOST CLOSELY RELATED TO HIPPOPOTAMUSES.

**25** THE ARMADILLO IS A TYPE OF LIZARD.

**26** ALL FISH HAVE GILLS.

**27** ANIMALS THAT EAT MAINLY FISH ARE CALLED CARNIVORES.

**28** MOTHS DON'T HAVE EYES.

**29** INSECTIVORES EAT BUGS.

**30** THE NAME "AARDVARK" COMES FROM THE AFRIKAANS WORD *ERDVARK*, WHICH MEANS "EARTH PIG."

CHECK YOUR ANSWERS ON PAGES 158–159.

# Chill OUT

WALRUS

**1** Where do emperor penguins live?
a. Antarctica
c. China
b. Brazil
d. Russia

**2** **True or false?** Both male and female walruses have tusks.

CARIBOU

**3** What adaptation makes polar bears great swimmers?
a. gills
c. white fur
b. flippers
d. webbed paws

**4** Which predators do gentoo penguins have to watch out for?
a. polar bears
b. orcas
c. tigers
d. eagles

**5** What do caribou eat during the winter?
a. lichen
b. ice
c. ants
d. pine needles

**6** What does a walrus do to survive in frigid water?
a. swims faster
b. uses seaweed as a blanket
c. slows its heartbeat
d. wears a sweater

GENTOO PENGUIN

**7** Where would an arctic fox take shelter during a blizzard?

a. in a tree
b. burrowed in the snow
c. underwater
d. with a colony of penguins

ARCTIC FOX

**8** Who sits on the emperor penguin's eggs?

a. the mother
b. the father
c. mom and dad take turns
d. no one; it buries its eggs

**9** True or false? Butterflies can't survive north of the U.S.–Canada border.

ARCTIC HARE

**10** Which of these hibernate in winter?

a. gopher tortoise
b. edible dormouse
c. horseshoe bat
d. all of the above

**11** Why do arctic hares have short ears?

a. to conserve heat
b. to hear better
c. to hide from vultures
d. as a fashion statement

BACTRIAN CAMEL

**12** How does the Bactrian camel of the Gobi, a desert in China, prepare for winter?

a. It migrates south.
b. It hibernates in the sand.
c. It grows a shaggy coat.
d. Nothing; there's no winter in the desert.

**13** Which creature can survive being frozen solid?

a. giraffe
b. kangaroo
c. seagull
d. wood frog

CHECK YOUR ANSWERS ON PAGES 158–159.

# DOGGONE IT!

**1** Which dog breed **runs** the fastest?

a. beagle
b. husky
c. poodle
d. greyhound

**2** What do you call a **domesticated dog** that lives like a wild animal?

a. werewolf
b. buster
c. mutt
d. feral

**3** True or false? Dogs can't continue to track a smell after it **rains.**

**4** In what year did the song "How Much Is That Doggie in the Window" first reach No. 1 on the **charts?**

a. 1933
b. 1953
c. 1983
d. 2003

**5** What does a **shih-tzu** look like?

a. big with curly hair
b. white with brown spots
c. small with long hair
d. large with fangs

A PACK OF
BORDER COLLIES

In the WILD

**6** What does the name "dachshund" mean in German?

a. sea dog
b. badger dog
c. shrimpy
d. hot dog

**7** True or false? You have more taste buds than a **dog**.

**8** How many dogs survived when the *Titanic* sank?

a. 0
b. 1
c. 3
d. 50

**9** What was the **cocker spaniel** originally bred to do?

a. hunt woodcock birds
b. guard the king
c. run races
d. pull sleds

**10** What are most bomb-sniffing dogs taught to do when they smell an **explosive**?

a. jump up and down
b. bark
c. dig a hole
d. sit down

**11** What color are newborn **Dalmatians?**

a. all white
b. all black
c. spotted
d. reddish brown

**12** True or false? All dogs can bark.

**13** Which of the following **dogs** is an excellent swimmer?

a. pug
b. basset hound
c. Labrador retriever
d. Pekingese

# GAME SHOW

## ULTIMATE ANIMAL CHALLENGE

**1** Which animal has been sent to outer space?
a. gecko
b. dog
c. monkey
d. all of the above

**2** Where do mother harp seals give birth?
a. on the ice
b. underwater
c. in a cave
d. on tropical islands

**3** TRUE OR FALSE?
Early European explorers thought manatees were mermaids.

**4** What breed of dog is Snoopy, from the *Peanuts* cartoon?
a. Chihuahua     c. husky
b. beagle        d. Maltese

**5** The velociraptor's long tail likely helped it balance while _____.
a. swimming
b. jumping and leaping
c. sleeping in trees
d. flying

**6** Where can you find wild peregrine falcons?
a. Africa
b. Australia
c. South America
d. all of the above

**7** What does a koala do to keep cool in hot weather?
a. hug a tree
b. jump in a lake
c. dig a hole
d. wear sunglasses

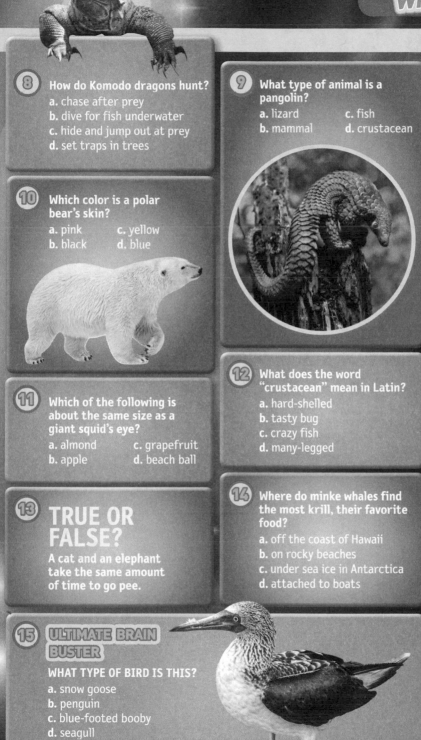

**8** How do Komodo dragons hunt?
a. chase after prey
b. dive for fish underwater
c. hide and jump out at prey
d. set traps in trees

**9** What type of animal is a pangolin?
a. lizard       c. fish
b. mammal       d. crustacean

**10** Which color is a polar bear's skin?
a. pink       c. yellow
b. black       d. blue

**11** Which of the following is about the same size as a giant squid's eye?
a. almond       c. grapefruit
b. apple       d. beach ball

**12** What does the word "crustacean" mean in Latin?
a. hard-shelled
b. tasty bug
c. crazy fish
d. many-legged

**13** TRUE OR FALSE?
A cat and an elephant take the same amount of time to go pee.

**14** Where do minke whales find the most krill, their favorite food?
a. off the coast of Hawaii
b. on rocky beaches
c. under sea ice in Antarctica
d. attached to boats

**15** ULTIMATE BRAIN BUSTER
WHAT TYPE OF BIRD IS THIS?
a. snow goose
b. penguin
c. blue-footed booby
d. seagull

CHECK YOUR ANSWERS ON PAGES 158–159.

# Wild WORLD

DESCENDING A SKI LIFT AT
AMDEN, SWITZERLAND

# Wild World of SPORTS

**1** What equipment is needed to play cricket?
- **a.** racket
- **b.** bat
- **c.** ankle weights
- **d.** swim fins

**2** Which sport is the national game of Pakistan?
- **a.** basketball
- **b.** water polo
- **c.** falconry
- **d.** field hockey

**3** **True or false?** Danica Patrick is an Irish gymnast.

DANICA PATRICK

**4** Which sport became part of the Summer Olympic Games in 1964?
- **a.** track and field
- **b.** volleyball
- **c.** rhythmic gymnastics
- **d.** swimming

**5** Which American sport is sometimes called gridiron in other countries?
- **a.** racquetball
- **b.** squash
- **c.** football
- **d.** fencing

**6** On which continent did rugby get its start?
- **a.** South America
- **b.** North America
- **c.** Australia
- **d.** Europe

RUGBY PLAYER

28

# Wild WORLD

**7** In Japan, which sport is played professionally by the Chunichi Dragons and the Tokyo Yakult Swallows?

a. tennis
b. soccer
c. basketball
d. baseball

CHUNICHI DRAGON FANS

**8** Pebble Beach, St. Andrews, Augusta, and Cape Kidnappers are famous spots to play which sport?

a. curling
b. golf
c. tennis
d. ice hockey

IROQUOIS STICK SPORT PLAYER

**9** The Cherokee, Seminole, and Choctaw people still play a double-stick version of which popular sport?

a. hockey
b. stickball
c. lacrosse
d. polo

**10** Which of the following was not a new Olympic event at the 2014 Winter Games in Sochi, Russia?

a. luge relay
b. ice dancing
c. snowboard slopestyle
d. ski half-pipe

**11** Tejo players in Colombia throw metal disks into a paper triangle filled with _____.

a. gunpowder
b. food coloring
c. rotten tomatoes
d. water balloons

**12** **True or false?** Table tennis is also known as *jai alai.*

TABLE TENNIS

**13** **True or false?** Players in the game of *kabaddi* have to hold their breath when on the opposing team's side of the field.

CHECK YOUR ANSWERS ON PAGES 159–160.

# ALPINE JOURNEY

**1** How many peaks higher than 13,000 feet (3,962 m) are in the Alps?
- **a.** 44
- **b.** 67
- **c.** 75
- **d.** 82

**2** Wooden homes or cottages in the Alps that have overhanging eaves are known as _____.
- **a.** buntings
- **b.** villas
- **c.** chalets
- **d.** bungalows

**3** In Germany and Austria, some glaciers are being _____.
- **a.** chopped up to make ice cubes
- **b.** wrapped to prevent them from melting
- **c.** made into bobsled courses
- **d.** melted to make bottled water

**4** When completed, Switzerland's Gotthard Base Tunnel will be _____.
- **a.** twice as long as the Brooklyn Bridge
- **b.** longer than the Channel Tunnel
- **c.** the world's longest railway tunnel
- **d.** both b and c

**5** How many people live in the Alps?
- **a.** 500,000
- **b.** 4 million
- **c.** 14 million
- **d.** 50 million

**6** What traditional crafts would you bring home as souvenirs from the Alps?
- **a.** watches
- **b.** chocolate
- **c.** cuckoo clocks
- **d.** all of the above

**7** True or false? The pyramidal bugle is a popular instrument to play in Alpine countries.

**8** **True or false?** Twister, Fondue, and Border Patrol are the names of mountain bike trails in the Alps.

**9** **Which mode of transportation is *not* a popular way to travel up the steep slopes of the Alps?**
a. funicular
b. cog railway
c. monorail
d. gondola

**10** **The Via Alpina is a hiking trail in the Alps that goes through how many countries?**
a. three
b. four
c. six
d. eight

**11** **Which local dessert would you be likely to find on a menu at a restaurant in the Alps?**
a. mango lassi
b. bilberry tart
c. baklava
d. peach pie

**12** **The Matterhorn—one of the highest peaks in the Alps—gets about how much snowfall each year?**
a. 15 feet (4.6 m)
b. 22 feet (6.7 m)
c. 29 feet (8.8 m)
d. 48 feet (14.6 m)

**13** **Endurance runners race how far in the Ultra-Trail du Mont-Blanc competition through the Alps?**
a. 20 miles (32 km)
b. 55 miles (89 km)
c. 104 miles (167 km)
d. 176 miles (283 km)

VIEW OF THE ALPINE VILLAGE OF BERCHTESGADEN IN GERMANY

CHECK YOUR ANSWERS ON PAGES 159–160. **31**

# Country Challenge

1. FINLAND IS KNOWN AS THE LAND OF A THOUSAND LAKES.

2. THERE ARE FIVE LANDLOCKED COUNTRIES IN THE WORLD.

3. LEGOS WERE INVENTED IN CHINA.

4. THE COUNTRY OF BRAZIL IS NAMED AFTER A TREE.

5. LEONARDO DA VINCI, MICHELANGELO, AND RAPHAEL ARE ALL FAMOUS ARTISTS FROM SPAIN.

6. BHUTAN IS KNOWN AS THE GOLF CAPITAL OF ASIA.

7. BELGIUM HAS MORE COMIC BOOK WRITERS PER SQUARE MILE THAN ANY OTHER COUNTRY.

8. MOUNTAINEERS CAN CLIMB EIGHT OF THE WORLD'S TEN TALLEST MOUNTAINS IN NEPAL.

9. CANADA'S NICKNAME IS THE HEXAGON.

10. THE NETHERLANDS EXPORTS MORE FLOWERS THAN ANY OTHER COUNTRY.

11. MALTA IS KNOWN AS THE GREAT RED ISLAND BECAUSE OF ITS SUNSETS.

12. MOROCCO IS ABOUT THE SAME SIZE AS RHODE ISLAND.

13. ARGENTINA IS HOME TO THE SOUTHERNMOST CITY ON EARTH.

14. SHOPAHOLICS CAN VISIT THE WORLD'S LARGEST SHOPPING STREET IN GERMANY.

15. VIETNAM WAS THE FIRST COUNTRY TO ELECT A FEMALE HEAD OF STATE.

**16** THE MAORI PEOPLE CALL NEW ZEALAND AOTEAROA, WHICH MEANS "THE LAND OF THE LONG WHITE CLOUD."

**17** MEXICO IS HOME TO MORE DEADLY SNAKES THAN ANY OTHER COUNTRY ON EARTH.

**18** REGGAE MUSIC ORIGINATED ON THE ISLAND OF JAMAICA.

**19** THE ISLANDS OF COMOROS, OFF THE COAST OF AFRICA, ARE KNOWN AS THE PERFUME ISLES.

**20** JAPAN HAS MORE VOLCANOES THAN ANY OTHER COUNTRY.

**21** THE UNITED STATES IS HOME TO THE WORLD'S LARGEST FILM STUDIO.

**22** FRANCE HAS HOSTED THE WINTER OLYMPICS MORE THAN ANY OTHER COUNTRY.

**23** RUSSIA HAS ABOUT THE SAME SURFACE AREA AS THE DWARF PLANET PLUTO.

**24** PERU'S INTERNATIONAL POTATO CENTER HAS PRESERVED ALMOST 5,000 VARIETIES OF SPUDS (POTATOES).

**25** A KIND OF CATTLE, THE SAOLA, LIVES IN COLOMBIA.

**26** PEOPLE IN SPAIN REGULARLY EAT TAPAS AND PINTXOS.

**27** BRAZIL HAS MORE PORTUGUESE SPEAKERS THAN PORTUGAL.

**28** URUGUAY TRACKS EVERY COW IN THE COUNTRY FROM BIRTH UNTIL IT IS SOLD FOR ITS MEAT.

**29** THERE ARE MORE THAN HALF A BILLION BIKES IN JAPAN.

**30** POLAND HAS MORE CASTLES PER SQUARE MILE THAN ANYWHERE ELSE ON EARTH.

CHECK YOUR ANSWERS ON PAGES 159–160.

# It's a SIGN!

**1** This sign in Iceland indicates a good viewing point to see what type of animals?

**a.** penguins **c.** seals
**b.** whales **d.** manatees

**2** In which country would you find this sign stating that dogs must be kept on a leash in the park?

**a.** Denmark
**b.** Chile
**c.** Japan
**d.** Kenya

**3** Signs in Newfoundland and Sweden warn drivers of collisions with what large animal?

**a.** lemurs
**b.** bobcats
**c.** tapirs
**d.** moose

**4** **True or false?** There are ice-skater crossing signs in the Maldives.

**5** You will see this road sign and traffic lights at a _____.

**a.** car ferry
**b.** railroad crossing
**c.** pedestrian bridge
**d.** toll booth

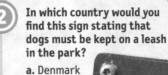

Hund i snor

**6** Where might you see this road sign?
a. Amazon rain forest
b. French seaside resort
c. Arabian desert
d. Australian outback

كثبان رملية
SAND DUNES

**7** **True or false?** Stop signs in different countries have the words *pare*, *arrêt*, and *berhenti*.

**8** In many countries around the globe, what punctuation mark is used on road signs to mean "warning"?
a. semicolon          c. exclamation point
b. question mark      d. comma

**9** On which road would you find this sign, meaning "no speed limit"?
a. Autobahn, Germany
b. Pacific Coast Highway, U.S.A.
c. Great Ocean Road, Australia
d. Milford Track, New Zealand

**10** You are most likely to see these two warning road signs outside _____.
a. a factory
b. a toy store
c. a school
d. an airport

ANSA EFTIR MÆR !

**11** **True or false?** Some New Zealand roads feature penguin crossing signs.

# WHAT'S FOR LUNCH?

**1** Yellow pea soup and taro root would be common **lunch** items in which city?

a. Beijing, China
b. Brisbane, Australia
c. Havana, Cuba
d. Rome, Italy

**2** True or false?
In **Kenya**, many lunches have ugali as a starch food to eat with a meat or fish stew.

**3** Which would be common lunch-menu options at a **restaurant** in Ukraine?

a. buckwheat and soup with potatoes
b. injera bread and beef with berbere sauce
c. ratatouille and rice
d. tofu and lo mein

**4** Japanese **lunch** eaters often enjoy kombu or nori with their rice. What are these?

a. berries
b. nuts
c. seaweed
d. fish

**5** Milanesa is a popular lunch for people in **Argentina**. What is it?

a. pasta with meat sauce
b. rabbit stew
c. meat dipped in egg and bread crumbs
d. a sandwich with tomato and mozzarella

**6** True or false?
**People in Mali often enjoy fried donuts for lunch.**

**7** True or false?
More than 200,000 lunch **boxes** are delivered daily to office workers in Mumbai, India.

36

**8** Schoolchildren would most likely be served **salmon**, fresh salad, and rice for school lunch in which country?

a. Pakistan    c. India
b. France    d. Ecuador

**9** Tiffins, **bento** boxes, and dosiraks are all types of what?

a. meat stews    c. vegetable soups
b. lunch boxes    d. serving utensils

**11** The **cemita**, a sandwich made from avocado, meat, cheese, pickled onions, and salsa, comes from which Latin American nation?

a. Bolivia
b. El Salvador
c. Brazil
d. Mexico

**10** You'd be most likely to enjoy sponge cake with custard for a lunchtime treat in which **city**?

a. London, England
b. Oslo, Norway
c. Rabat, Morocco
d. Ulaanbaatar, Mongolia

CHECK YOUR ANSWERS ON PAGES 159–160.

# Super CELEBRATIONS

**1** During which Hindu holiday do people light candles and lamps filled with oil?
- **a.** Janmashtami
- **b.** Diwali
- **c.** Raksha Bandhan
- **d.** Holi

**2** On Christmas Eve, people in which country pass around *oplatek*, a paper-thin wafer featuring a Nativity scene?
- **a.** Uruguay
- **b.** Greece
- **c.** Norway
- **d.** Poland

CANDLE LIGHT

**3** On which day does the oldest daughter in Swedish families bring saffron buns and hot coffee to her parents in bed?
- **a.** Christmas Day
- **b.** New Year's Day
- **c.** Feast Day of Santa Lucia
- **d.** her birthday

**4** At midnight on New Year's Eve, people in Spain do what as the clock chimes the hour?
- **a.** eat one grape
- **b.** yodel
- **c.** set off firecrackers
- **d.** cough

**5** True or false? People in the Philippines wear polka dots on New Year's Eve.

**6** People of which faith celebrate Tu B'shevat by planting trees and eating fruit?
- **a.** Christian
- **b.** Buddhist
- **c.** Muslim
- **d.** Jewish

CLOCK

**7** During which holiday do people celebrate their African heritage by lighting candles of different colors?
**a.** Hanukkah      **c.** Eid al-Adha
**b.** Kwanzaa       **d.** Carnivale

**8** **True or false?** Women in Japan give the men in their lives chocolate on Valentine's Day.

CHOCOLATES

**9** On the holiday of Wesak, people often release caged birds to celebrate whose birthday?
**a.** Muhammad's
**b.** Jesus's
**c.** Buddha's
**d.** Gandhi's

BAGPIPE PLAYER

**10** Which celebration involves bagpipe music, jigs, and the color green?
**a.** St. Nicholas Day
**b.** St. Patrick's Day
**c.** St. Lucia's Day
**d.** Day of the Dead

**11** **True or false?** People in China usually wear yellow for good luck at their Chinese New Year celebrations.

CHECK YOUR ANSWERS ON PAGES 159–160.

# MAP MANIA!
# WHERE IN THE WORLD

Identify these countries from their flags and currencies.

① China

② United Kingdom

③ Sweden

④ India

⑤ Turkey

6

7

8

ARCTIC OCEAN

H

EUROPE

I

A

J

S

C

D

K

PACIFIC OCEAN

AFRICA

E

INDIAN OCEAN

F

ANTARCTICA

**12–22**

MATCH EACH OF THESE COUNTRIES TO ITS CORRECT LOCATION ON THE MAP.

9

10

11

CHECK YOUR ANSWERS ON PAGES 159–160.

**41**

# GAME SHOW

# ULTIMATE GEOGRAPHY CHALLENGE

**1** Which three countries' national soccer teams are named after elephants?
a. Sri Lanka, Germany, India
b. Guinea, Thailand, Côte d'Ivoire
c. Japan, Burkina Faso, South Africa
d. Uganda, Cuba, Malaysia

**2** TRUE OR FALSE?
There are more than 700 indigenous languages spoken in Papua New Guinea.

**3** In which country are Easter eggs delivered by a cuckoo bird instead of a bunny?
a. Switzerland       c. Bulgaria
b. Portugal          d. Mexico

**4** Which country's nickname is Sunny Side of the Alps?
a. France       c. Slovenia
b. Italy        d. Greece

**5** In which country do drivers often see yellow-and-black kangaroo road signs?
a. India        c. Australia
b. Tonga        d. South Africa

**6** Which country is part of the "hinge" area linking northern and southern Africa?
a. Tunisia      c. Maldives
b. Libya        d. Cameroon

**7** Which of the following items were banned from being brought into the 2014 World Cup stadiums in Brazil?
a. umbrellas
b. huge flags and flag poles
c. cameras
d. all of the above

**8** Where is *som tum*, a spicy salad featuring papaya, often eaten with sticky rice for lunch?

a. Pakistan      c. Suriname
b. Thailand      d. Bulgaria

**9** Which mountainous country is known as the Kingdom of the Sky?

a. Angola       c. El Salvador
b. China        d. Lesotho

**10** TRUE OR FALSE?

Japan is home to more children than pets.

**11** Which continent is home to national soccer teams named after cranes, swallows, eagles, and falcons?

a. North America
b. Africa
c. South America
d. Europe

**12** *Sepak takraw*, a game that's a mix of karate and volleyball, originated in which region?

a. southeastern Asia
b. northern Europe
c. southern Africa
d. central North America

**13** Where do people celebrate midsummer by wearing flower wreaths in their hair and eating potatoes and herring?

a. Albania      c. South Korea
b. Sweden       d. Brazil

**14** TRUE OR FALSE?

People in France celebrate the end of the 12 Days of Christmas by eating king cake.

**15** ULTIMATE BRAIN BUSTER

Which of these road signs will you probably never see in North America?

a.      b.      c.      d.

CHECK YOUR ANSWERS ON PAGES 159–160.

43

# Pop CULTURE

BEN STILLER IN THE FILM *NIGHT AT THE MUSEUM: BATTLE OF THE SMITHSONIAN*

# '90s NOVELTIES

**WILL SMITH**

**1** Actor Will Smith's first role was in which famous TV comedy?
a. *Full House*
b. *Saved by the Bell*
c. *The Fresh Prince of Bel-Air*
d. *ALF*

**2** The Tamagotchi was a digital pet that could do each of the following except _____ .
a. eat
b. get sick
c. sleep
d. run

**3** Which movie was the biggest blockbuster of the 1990s?
a. *Titanic*
b. *The Lion King*
c. *Men in Black*
d. *Jurassic Park*

**TAMAGOTCHI**

**4** True or false?
Grunge was a gritty style of rock music that started in Seattle, Washington, U.S.A.

**5** Which would you wear if you wanted to look cool in the 1990s?
a. a shirt with shoulder pads
b. a poodle skirt
c. a flannel shirt
d. a white polyester suit

**6** Which Southern California, U.S.A., zip code became famous thanks to a television show about teens?
a. 94101
b. 90210
c. 92093
d. 92262

**7** Which singer isn't one of the Spice Girls?
a. Sporty
b. Pink
c. Ginger
d. Baby

SPICE GIRLS

**8** What animal was the "spokesperson" for the fast-food chain Taco Bell?
a. African elephant
b. Chihuahua
c. koala
d. giant panda

**9** The Spanish band Los del Rio started a dance craze with a song called _____.
a. "Macarena"
b. "Twist"
c. "Party Rock Anthem"
d. "The Hustle"

**10** What farmer-friendly clothing was popular with both men and women in the 1990s?
a. wide-brimmed hats
b. worker gloves
c. overalls
d. platform sneakers

**11** True or false?
Pikachu was a character from the Donkey Kong video game series.

ROLLERBLADES

**12** In the 1990s, many people started to wear Rollerblades instead of what footwear?
a. ice skates
b. moon boots
c. roller skates
d. Kangoo Jumps

**13** Which boy band did *not* make its debut in the 1990s?
a. Backstreet Boys
b. *NSYNC
c. One Direction
d. 98 Degrees

# THERE'S AN APP FOR THAT

**1** Which *Shrek* character is the star of a special-edition **Fruit Ninja** app?

a. Donkey
b. Puss in Boots
c. Gingerbread Man
d. Pinocchio

**2** Tiffi, Odus, and the Bubblegum Troll star in which **video** game?

a. *Angry Birds: Star Wars II*
b. *Temple Run*
c. *Despicable Me: Minion Rush*
d. *Candy Crush Saga*

**3** To defeat his enemies, the Hungry Sumo must eat a **lot** of _____.

a. rice
b. pizza
c. pancakes
d. celery

**4** Which app allows you to animate any photo with a talking **mouth**?

a. Doodle Jump
b. Jet Ball
c. FEZ
d. ChatterPix Kids

**5** True or false? In *Cut the Rope: Time Travel*, Om Nom travels to the **Victorian Age.**

**6** The **object** of *Clumsy Ninja* is to help the character find his _____.

a. friend
b. home
c. pet
d. hat

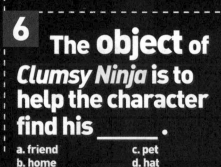

**7** In which **Toca** app can you perform scientific experiments?

a. Toca Pet Doctor
b. Toca Kitchen Monsters
c. Toca Lab
d. Toca Builders

**8** You can advance your level in *Despicable Me: Minion Rush* by collecting what **type** of food?

a. fruit
b. candy
c. hot dogs
d. vegetables

**9** In *Star Wars: Tiny Death Star*, players must help which character build the **Death Star?**

a. Princess Leia
b. Darth Vader
c. Jabba the Hutt
d. Han Solo

**10** What city must players help Spider-Man **save** in *Spider-Man: Total Mayhem*?

a. Rome, Italy
b. New York City, U.S.A.
c. Istanbul, Turkey
d. Toronto, Canada

**11** True or false?

Notch is the **nickname** for Markus Persson, who is credited with creating *Minecraft – Pocket Edition.*

**12** What do players use to buy parts needed to build a **transformer** in *Transformers Construct-Bots*?

a. coins
b. crabby patties
c. barrels
d. rivets

# Monster MASH

**GODZILLA**

**1** What character from the Twilight series is a werewolf?

a. Renesmee   c. Jessica
b. Jacob      d. Carlisle

**2** True or false?
Godzilla lives in a volcano.

**3** Which food would you traditionally use to ward off a vampire?

a. garlic   c. pepper
b. ginger   d. oregano

**VAMPIRE**

**4** The Headless Horseman terrorized citizens in which U.S. community?

a. Los Angeles, California
b. Sleepy Hollow, New York
c. Boston, Massachusetts
d. Austin, Texas

**5** In the Harry Potter series, Azkaban was guarded by creatures called _____.

a. Dementors
b. Voldemort
c. Muggles
d. wizards

**GRINCH**

**6** Why was the Grinch so mean?

a. He hated being green.
b. His heart was two sizes too small.
c. He wasn't allowed in Whoville.
d. He disliked living in a cave.

**7** What famous structure did King Kong climb after escaping from captivity?
a. the Tower of London
b. the Leaning Tower of Pisa
c. the Empire State Building
d. the Eiffel Tower

**8** True or false?
In the novel *Frankenstein*, the author never states how the monster is brought to life.

**9** In what book does Max play with monsters while wearing a wolf costume?
a. *Where the Wild Things Are*
b. *The BFG*
c. *The Witches*
d. *Monsters in the Attic*

**10** What is the Loch Ness monster's nickname?
a. Marge
b. Nessie
c. Nora
d. Hermione

**11** Elsa's monster in *Frozen* is called _____ .
a. Snowy
b. Jack Frost
c. Marshmallow
d. Hans

**12** In the original *Shrek* film, Princess Fiona is held hostage by _____ .
a. an ogre
b. a fire-breathing dragon
c. the Big Bad Wolf
d. the Headless Horseman

SHREK

**13** In which city do the characters from *Monsters, Inc.* live?
a. Monstropolis
b. Gotham City
c. Metropolis
d. Smallville

CHECK YOUR ANSWERS ON PAGES 161–162.

# TRUE or FALSE?
# Blockbuster Books

**1** *JOURNEY TO THE CENTER OF THE EARTH* AND *THE TIME MACHINE* WERE WRITTEN BY THE SAME AUTHOR.

**2** *HEIDI*, BY JOHANNA SPYRI, TAKES PLACE IN THE HIMALAYA.

**3** IN *JAMES AND THE GIANT PEACH*, THE MAIN CHARACTER'S PARENTS ARE GOBBLED UP BY A RHINOCEROS.

**4** PIPPI LONGSTOCKING IS KNOWN FOR HER CURLY HAIR.

**5** *THE LITTLE PRINCE* TAKES PLACE IN THE GOBI, A DESERT IN ASIA.

**6** IN *ARTEMIS FOWL*, THE MAIN CHARACTER CAPTURES A FAIRY.

**7** *THE MAZE OF BONES* IS THE FIRST BOOK OF THE WESTING GAMES SERIES.

**8** MRS. FRISBY, THE TITLE CHARACTER IN *MRS. FRISBY AND THE RATS OF NIMH*, IS A CROW.

**9** IN *FRINDLE*, NICK ALLEN CHANGES THE WORD "PEN" TO "FRINDLE."

**10** CAPTAIN UNDERPANTS IS THE ALIAS OF A SCHOOL PRINCIPAL.

**11** IN *TALES OF A FOURTH GRADE NOTHING*, PETER HATCHER HAS TO DEAL WITH HIS ANNOYING KID SISTER, RAMONA.

**12** *THE DIARY OF ANNE FRANK* IS A TRUE STORY.

**13** HAILEY AND CLAIRE DISCOVER A MERMAID IN *AQUAMARINE*.

**14** IN *HOOT*, THE CONSTRUCTION OF A PANCAKE HOUSE THREATENS TO DESTROY A HERD OF PIGS THAT LIVE ON THE SITE.

**15** CHARACTERS FROM BOOKS COME TO LIFE IN *INKHEART*.

**16** STANLEY YELNATS'S NICKNAME IN *HOLES* IS X-RAY.

**17** IN *THE PHANTOM TOLLBOOTH*, DICTIONOPOLIS IS A LAND OF NUMBERS.

**18** IN *THE HUNGER GAMES*, PEETA'S FAMILY OWNS A BAKERY.

**19** PERCY JACKSON AND HIS FELLOW HALF-BLOOD HEROES BATTLE THE OLYMPIANS IN *THE LAST OLYMPIAN*.

**20** THE PANTS IN THE TITLE *THE SISTERHOOD OF THE TRAVELING PANTS* ARE A PAIR OF JEANS.

**21** IN *CHARLIE AND THE CHOCOLATE FACTORY*, VIOLET BEAUREGARDE'S SPECIAL SKILL IS WHISTLING.

**22** THE DOG IN THE BOOK *SHILOH* IS A BEAGLE.

**23** IN *BECAUSE OF WINN-DIXIE*, OPAL NAMES A DOG AFTER A SUPERMARKET.

**24** PIGLET'S CATCHPHRASE IS "GOOD GOLLY" IN *WINNIE-THE-POOH*.

**25** *JUMANJI* IS ABOUT AN UNUSUAL BOARD GAME.

**26** IN *MR. POPPER'S PENGUINS*, THE POPPERS KEEP THEIR FIRST PENGUIN IN THE REFRIGERATOR.

**27** MARY LENNOX SURVIVES AN OUTBREAK OF CHICKEN POX IN *THE SECRET GARDEN*.

**28** WILBUR IS BEFRIENDED BY A SPIDER IN *CHARLOTTE'S WEB*.

**29** IN *HOW TO EAT FRIED WORMS*, BILLY EATS WORMS BECAUSE HE LIKES THE WAY THEY TASTE.

**30** HARRY POTTER HAS A SCAR IN THE SHAPE OF A HEART.

CHECK YOUR ANSWERS ON PAGES 161–162.

# Tune IN

THE BEATLES

**1** Which song was recorded by the classic rock group The Beatles?

a. "(I Can't Get No) Satisfaction"
b. "Jailhouse Rock"
c. "Proud Mary"
d. "Yellow Submarine"

**2** Who is not a member of One Direction?

a. Harry Styles    c. Nathan Sykes
b. Liam Payne    d. Niall Horan

**3** Which smash hit by Lorde was No. 1 on the Billboard music charts in 2013?

a. "Tennis Court"    c. "Team"
b. "Royals"    d. "No Better"

LORDE

**4** "Clap along if you know what happiness is to you" is a lyric from what megahit from the *Despicable Me 2* soundtrack?

a. "Roar"
b. "I Knew You Were Trouble"
c. "Happy"
d. "With You"

**5** Which sun- and surf-loving band scored a hit with the song "California Girls" in 1965?

a. The Doors
b. The Beach Boys
c. The Searchers
d. The Who

**6** Which reality-show host is also a singer?

a. Ryan Seacrest    c. Nick Cannon
b. Carson Daly    d. Cat Deeley

**7** Ed Sheeran and Taylor Swift teamed up for what duet?

a. "Everything Has Changed"    c. "Just Give Me a Reason"
b. "The Way"                   d. "Stay"

JENNIFER LOPEZ

**8** True or false?
Jennifer Lopez's
first pop album was
named *On the 6*.

**9** What song did not appear on Katy Perry's *Teenage Dream* album?

a. "Firework"
b. "California Gurls"
c. "Roar"
d. "Last Friday Night (T.G.I.F.)"

**10** Which singer was not a performer on Disney's *The Mickey Mouse Club*?

a. Pink                  c. Justin Timberlake
b. Christina Aguilera    d. Britney Spears

**11** The song "Cups (When I'm Gone)" was performed by which actress in the movie *Pitch Perfect*?

a. Anna Kendrick
b. Brittany Snow
c. Rebel Williams
d. Alexis Knapp

**12** Which "amazing" artist performed at the Super Bowl in 2014?

a. Pharrell Williams
b. Bruno Mars
c. Justin Timberlake
d. Drake

ELVIS PRESLEY

**13** Elvis Presley recorded a song that had which dog in the title?

a. Scottish terrier
b. hound dog
c. pug
d. shar-pei

# TRUE or FALSE?

# Ready, Set, Action!

1. *NIGHT AT THE MUSEUM: SECRET OF THE TOMB* TAKES PLACE IN A MUSEUM IN ROME.

2. EMMA WATSON PLAYED BELLA SWAN IN THE TWILIGHT SERIES.

3. MALEFICENT IS A FAIRY.

4. IN *THE NUT JOB*, SURLY'S SIDEKICK IS A RAT.

5. A GROUP OF KIDS TRY TO HELP AN ALIEN FIND ITS WAY HOME IN *EARTH TO ECHO*.

6. IN *DOLPHIN TALE 2*, SAWYER NELSON AND HIS FRIENDS TRY TO RESCUE A DOLPHIN NAMED SUMMER.

7. THOR GOT HIS SUPERPOWERS BY VOLUNTEERING FOR A MILITARY EXPERIMENT.

8. THE ISLAND OF BERK FROM THE HOW TO TRAIN YOUR DRAGON SERIES IS POPULATED BY GLADIATORS.

9. BATMAN JOINS FORCES WITH IRON MAN IN *THE LEGO MOVIE*.

10. E.T. EATS M&MS IN THE MOVIE.

11. *STAR WARS: EPISODE 1* SHOWS LUKE SYKWALKER AS A YOUNG BOY.

12. THE TEENAGE MUTANT NINJA TURTLES' FAVORITE SNACK IS HAMBURGERS.

13. THE WABAC MACHINE FROM *MR. PEABODY & SHERMAN* IS A TIME-TRAVEL MACHINE.

14. HERMEY THE ELF FROM *RUDOLPH THE RED-NOSED REINDEER* WANTS TO BE A VETERINARIAN.

15. BRUCE WAYNE IS THE SECRET IDENTITY OF CAPTAIN AMERICA.

**16** IN *GNOMEO & JULIET*, THE GARDENS OF BOTH GNOMES ARE NEARLY DESTROYED BY A LAWN MOWER.

**17** MUMBLE IS UNABLE TO SING IN *HAPPY FEET*.

**18** PO MUST PROTECT GONGMEN CITY FROM A VULTURE IN *KUNG FU PANDA 2*.

**19** IN *THE LORAX*, TED GOES IN SEARCH OF A TREE TO WIN OVER AUDREY.

**20** IN *THE WIZARD OF OZ*, DOROTHY DESTROYS THE WICKED WITCH OF THE WEST BY THROWING WATER ON HER.

**21** IN *FINDING NEMO*, NEMO'S DAD, MARLIN, IS A TYPE OF FISH CALLED A MARLIN.

**22** IN THE CLASSIC MOVIE *THE GOONIES*, A GROUP OF KIDS GO IN SEARCH OF A PIRATE'S TREASURE.

**23** IN *RATATOUILLE*, A RAT NAMED REMY DREAMS OF BECOMING A CHEF.

**24** THE MOVIE *RANGO* TAKES PLACE IN A DESERT.

**25** SHREK MAKES A DEAL HE REGRETS WITH THE BIG BAD WOLF IN *SHREK FOREVER AFTER*.

**26** IN *PARANORMAN*, NORMAN BABOCK HAS THE ABILITY TO SPEAK TO THE DEAD.

**27** IN THE MOVIE *ELF*, BUDDY REVEALS THAT SINGING CHRISTMAS CAROLS WILL MAKE SANTA'S SLEIGH FLY.

**28** THE FLDSMDFR IS RESPONSIBLE FOR CREATING THE FOODIMALS IN *CLOUDY WITH A CHANCE OF MEATBALLS 2*.

**29** IN *THE HUNGER GAMES: CATCHING FIRE*, PREVIOUS WINNERS OF THE GAMES MUST FIGHT ONE ANOTHER.

**30** IN *TRANSFORMERS: AGE OF EXTINCTION*, CADE PURCHASES A TRUCK THAT TURNS OUT TO BE OPTIMUS PRIME.

# GAME SHOW

# ULTIMATE POP CULTURE CHALLENGE

**1** Popular in the 1990s, Beanie Babies were plush animals stuffed with _____.
- **a.** sand
- **b.** rocks
- **c.** lima beans
- **d.** plastic beads

**2** Who scored a hit with the song "Counting Stars" in 2014?
- **a.** Carrie Underwood
- **b.** OneRepublic
- **c.** Adele
- **d.** Elton John

**3** Which character would you expect to find in the game app Temple Run: Brave?
- **a.** Hans
- **b.** Merida
- **c.** Nemo
- **d.** Kermit

**4** In the game app Where's My Water, what type of reptile is Swampy?
- **a.** gecko
- **b.** Komodo dragon
- **c.** alligator
- **d.** iguana

**5** In Greek mythology, the Minotaur is a creature that has the body of a human and the head of a _____ .
- **a.** horse
- **b.** lion
- **c.** chicken
- **d.** bull

**6** TRUE OR FALSE?

*Titanic* characters Jack and Rose are based on real people.

**7**

Mia Thermopolis discovers that her father was the prince of the fictional country of _____ in *The Princess Diaries*.

a. Genovia
b. Narnia
c. Camelot
d. Gondor

**8** In the movie *Frankenweenie*, what is the name of Victor's dog?

a. Fido
b. Happy
c. Sparky
d. Spot

**9** What type of animal is Rikki-Tikki-Tavi from *The Jungle Book*?

a. goat
b. snake
c. mongoose
d. horse

**10** What performer has never been a judge on *The Voice*?

a. Keith Urban
b. Shakira
c. Gwen Stefani
d. Usher

**11** Which toy was launched in the 1990s?

a. Rubik's Cube
b. Furby
c. Cabbage Patch Kid
d. Easy-Bake Oven

**12** In the movie *Planes*, Dusty is a crop dusting plane with a fear of _____.

a. spiders
b. heights
c. lightning
d. dirt

**13** Kids transform into animals in which popular book series?

a. Goosebumps
b. Magic Tree House
c. Animorphs
d. Little House on the Prairie

**14 ULTIMATE CHALLENGE** What hairstyle was all the rage in the 1990s?

a. The beehive
b. The Rachel
c. The bob
d. The pixie

# Get OUTSIDE

HERE COME THE CUB SCOUTS.

GRIZZLY BEARS AT KATMAI NATIONAL PARK AND PRESERVE, ALASKA, U.S.A.

# Seasons of CHANGE

**1** Why do we experience seasons on Earth?
   **a.** Earth is tilted on its axis as it travels around the sun.
   **b.** Light from stars heats and cools the planet.
   **c.** The moon's orbit pulls the planet in different directions.
   **d.** Light is reflected from the moon half the year.

**2** Which tree dropped this autumn leaf?
   **a.** pine      **c.** ash
   **b.** maple     **d.** willow

HIGHLAND GAMES

**3** If you live in Australia, in which month is the winter solstice?
   **a.** June       **c.** March
   **b.** September  **d.** December

**4** In which season are the Highland Games held in Scotland?
   **a.** spring     **c.** autumn
   **b.** summer     **d.** winter

RACCOON

**5** Nordkapp, Norway, is the northernmost point of mainland Europe. In the summer, what time does the sun set there?
   **a.** 7 p.m.      **c.** 2 a.m.
   **b.** midnight    **d.** never

**6** True or false?
   Raccoons hibernate during the winter.

PUMPKINS

**7** Where was the world's tallest snowman—which was actually a snowwoman—measuring 122 feet, 1 inch (37.2 m), built?

a. Moscow, Russia
b. Santiago, Chile
c. Bethel, Maine, U.S.A.
d. Antarctica

**8** In North America, what time of year are pumpkins ready to be harvested?

a. midsummer
b. spring
c. early autumn
d. late winter

**9** The "dog days of summer" are when _____ .

a. Sirius, the Dog Star, is high in the sky
b. everyone is so hot that they pant like dogs
c. thunderstorms that sound like growling dogs occur
d. it's the best time of year to get a puppy

**10** What should you use tongs for when cooking at a summer barbecue?

a. starting the fire
b. flipping food on the grill
c. seasoning the food
d. eating corn on the cob

**11** How many seeds does one sunflower produce?

a. 1
b. 2 to 15
c. about 50
d. more than 500

**12** In which season is lightning most likely to strike?

a. winter
b. spring
c. summer
d. fall

SUNFLOWER

CHECK YOUR ANSWERS ON PAGES 162–163.

# STORM CENTRAL

**1** **What is sleet?**

a. acid rain
c. frozen rain
b. thick snow
d. high winds

**2** **The summit of Mount Wai'ale'ale is one of the rainiest places on Earth, getting about 350 days of rain each year. Where is the mountain?**

a. Siberia
c. Hawaii
b. Indonesia
d. the Alps

**3** **What are you afraid of if you have astraphobia?**

a. thunder and lightning
c. falling rocks
b. snow
d. tornadoes

**4** **What makes a tree more likely to fall during a storm?**

a. fungi on the wood
c. tall height
b. broken roots
d. all of the above

**5** **True or false?** **Wind chill affects only living things.**

**6** **True or false? A rain of frogs is impossible.**

**7** **Where do the fastest winds on Earth form?**

a. inside a tornado
c. on top of mountains
b. over the ocean
d. all of the above

**8** **What should you do if you're caught outside in a sandstorm with no shelter?**

a. stand still
b. scream as loud as you can
c. tie a cloth over your nose and mouth
d. take off your shoes

**9** **Which weather effect picks up Dorothy's house in *The Wizard of Oz*?**

a. firestorm          c. thunderstorm
b. tornado            d. hurricane

**10** **True or false?** **Lightning flashes can travel from the ground up to a cloud.**

**11** **What causes a geomagnetic storm?**

a. eruptions on the sun    c. volcanoes erupting
b. comets flying by        d. hurricanes

**12** **About how many lightning bolts strike Earth each second?**

a. 7          c. 5,000
b. 100        d. 1 million

**13** **Red rain occasionally falls on Europe. What causes the red color?**

a. blood          c. bacteria
b. desert dust    d. ketchup

**14** **True or false?** **Snow can't fall if the temperature on the ground is above freezing.**

A TORNADO ROARS ACROSS THE
GREAT PLAINS.

CHECK YOUR ANSWERS ON PAGES 162–163.

# Great GARDENS

1. **Which ruler built the gardens at the Palace of Versailles in France?**
   a. Emperor Charlemagne
   b. Marie Antoinette
   c. King Louis XIV
   d. Queen Elizabeth II

2. **What is the word for a garden devoted to trees?**
   a. arboretum
   b. leaf zoo
   c. floriform
   d. tree-topia

3. **True or false?**
   Flowers can't grow in a desert.

4. **Which artist painted views of the water lilies in the gardens of Giverny, France?**
   a. Pablo Picasso
   b. Jackson Pollock
   c. Claude Monet
   d. Georgia O'Keefe

5. **True or false?**
   Most Japanese Zen gardens contain no plants at all.

VERSAILLES, FRANCE

GIVERNY, FRANCE

**GARDEN FLOWERS**

**6** Which of the following was one of the Seven Wonders of the Ancient World?

a. Garden of Eden
b. Field of Dreams
c. Infinite Meadow
d. Hanging Gardens of Babylon

**7** True or false?
Roses are the only flowers in the White House Rose Garden in Washington, D.C., U.S.A.

**8** A shrub that's trimmed to look like a figure or an animal is called a _____ .

a. living statue
b. topiary
c. green thumb
d. shrubathon

**9** Which plants form the walls of the Garden Maze at Luray Caverns in Virginia, U.S.A.?

a. coniferous trees
b. twisted vines
c. flowering bushes
d. thick moss

**10** Which country first developed the art of growing bonsai trees?

a. Japan
b. India
c. China
d. Russia

**ANIMAL-SHAPED SHRUB**

**11** Which book is about a little girl who befriends a disabled boy?

a. *The Secret Garden*
b. *Flowers for Algernon*
c. *Anne of Green Gables*
d. *The Maze Runner*

**BONSAI TREE**

**CHECK YOUR ANSWERS ON PAGES 162–163.**

# ROLLING DOWN RIVER

**1** Which **river** carries the largest volume of water?

a. Amazon
b. Yangtze
c. Nile
d. Mississippi

**2** How did most early steamboats **move** through the water?

a. propellers
b. long poles
c. large paddlewheels
d. sails

**3** True or false? The water of the Colorado River rarely reaches the **ocean**.

**4** Which term is not a **word** for a small river?

a. creek
b. brook
c. stream
d. peninsula

**5** People of the _____ religion consider the Ganges River to be sacred.

a. Jewish
b. Christian
c. Hindu
d. Mormon

**6** True or false? In the sport of rowing, everyone in the boat has to **paddle**.

**7** Which **book** includes a trip down the Mississippi River?

a. *The Adventures of Huckleberry Finn*
b. *Charlotte's Web*
c. *The Hobbit*
d. *A Wrinkle in Time*

AERIAL VIEW OF A EUROPEAN RIVER IN SUMMER

**8** What adaptation helps a river otter **swim** quickly?

a. forked tail
b. gills
c. fin on its back
d. webbed feet

**9** **Where** is the Mekong River?

a. South America
b. Southeast Asia
c. Canada
d. Europe

**10** It is **safe** to drink river water _____.

a. when it has no smell
b. if you have boiled it
c. if it looks clear
d. if water lilies are growing in it

**11** When **farmers** use river water for irrigation, they are _____.

a. washing cars
b. filling swimming pools
c. watering crops
d. dancing in the rain

**12** Which **animal** lives in the Congo River in Africa?

a. hippopotamus
b. piranha
c. penguin
d. octopus

**13** True or false? Ancient Egyptians dug the **Nile River** out of a dry desert.

**14** Which **river** animal may already be **extinct**?

a. common snapping turtle
b. great blue heron
c. Chinese river dolphin
d. Australian crocodile

**15** Why do most dams have a **system** of gates called locks?

a. to keep seaweed out
b. to generate power
c. to help fish migrate
d. to get boats from one water level to another

CHECK YOUR ANSWERS ON PAGES 162–163.

# ROCKIN' REDWOODS

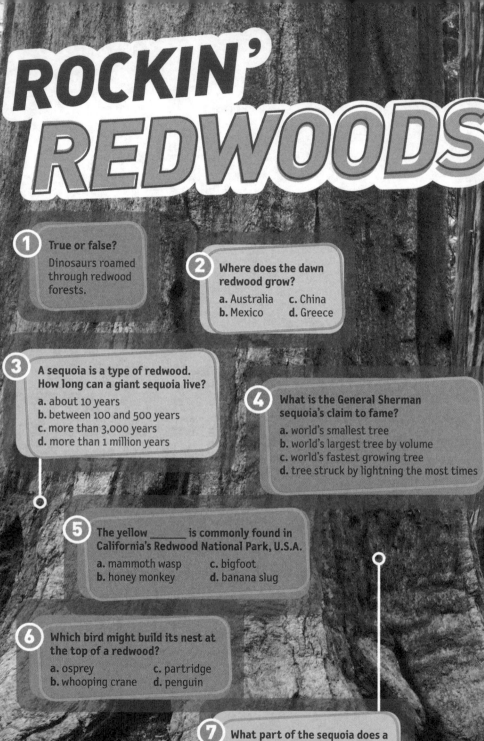

**1** True or false?
Dinosaurs roamed through redwood forests.

**2** Where does the dawn redwood grow?
a. Australia  c. China
b. Mexico  d. Greece

**3** A sequoia is a type of redwood. How long can a giant sequoia live?
a. about 10 years
b. between 100 and 500 years
c. more than 3,000 years
d. more than 1 million years

**4** What is the General Sherman sequoia's claim to fame?
a. world's smallest tree
b. world's largest tree by volume
c. world's fastest growing tree
d. tree struck by lightning the most times

**5** The yellow _____ is commonly found in California's Redwood National Park, U.S.A.
a. mammoth wasp  c. bigfoot
b. honey monkey  d. banana slug

**6** Which bird might build its nest at the top of a redwood?
a. osprey  c. partridge
b. whooping crane  d. penguin

**7** What part of the sequoia does a Douglas squirrel love to eat?
a. needles  c. bark
b. cones  d. roots

**8 True or false?**
A tree in Sequoia National Park, U.S.A., has a tunnel in its trunk that cars can drive through.

**9 What did the traditional homes of Native Americans living in redwood forests look like?**
a. rectangular houses built with redwood planks
b. tree houses
c. teepees made of deer hide and branches
d. metal domes

**10 True or false?**
Cutting down any redwood is illegal.

**11 Which U.S. national park is home to several groves of sequoia?**
a. Yellowstone
b. Everglades
c. Yosemite
d. Grand Teton

**12 How many people visit Sequoia National Park each year?**
a. fewer than 100
b. about 1,000
c. 25,000 to 50,000
d. about 1 million

**13 How does fog help redwoods survive?**
a. confuses bats
b. stops lightning
c. provides water
d. all of the above

**14 True or false?**
Most giant sequoias survive forest fires.

SEQUOIA NATIONAL FOREST, CALIFORNIA, U.S.A.

# COOL CAVES

**1** What do you call a **person** who explores caves?

a. rock diver
b. maniac
c. spelunker
d. dark knight

**2** **Caves** can form when lava flows through Earth. Which natural **disaster** may form lava-tube caves?

a. volcanic eruption
b. earthquake
c. sandstorm
d. tornado

**3** About how long does it take for a **stalactite** to grow 1 inch (2.5 cm)?

a. 1 year
b. 25 years
c. 200 years
d. 1 million years

**4** **Guano** is a material commonly found in caves. What is it?

a. ancient fossil
b. bat poop
c. crystal
d. poison gas

**5** Where is Mammoth Cave, the longest known cave in the **world**?

a. Alaska, U.S.A.
b. Delhi, India
c. Sahara desert
d. Kentucky, U.S.A.

**6** What is a **troglobite**?

a. a type of stalagmite
b. any creature that lives in a cave
c. a cave rock containing gold
d. a cave-dwelling baby dragon

**7** True or false? All **bats** sleep in caves.

**8** Where in a cave could you find rare **cave** pearls?

a. inside a cave oyster
b. in a cave pool
c. in a pirate's treasure chest
d. stuck to the ceiling

**9** What animal lives in Russia's Krubera Cave, the **deepest** known cave in the world?

a. whales
b. beetles
c. hummingbirds
d. all of the above

**10** True or false? Touching a stalactite could make it stop **growing.**

**11** What are natural cave **crystals** made of?

a. minerals
b. plastic
c. glass
d. magic

**12** What did early humans paint on the walls of Lascaux **caves** in France?

a. horses
b. wolves
c. rhinoceros
d. all of the above

**13** Which **cave** creature creates strings of lights that hang from the ceiling?

a. bats
b. salamanders
c. bears
d. glowworms

**14** True or false? Some cave-dwelling **fish** have no eyes.

NEPTUNE'S CAVE, SARDINIA, ITALY

CHECK YOUR ANSWERS ON PAGES 162–163.

# MAP MANIA!

# NATURE MADE

NORTH
AMERICA

● D
● F

ATLANTIC
OCEAN

PACIFIC
OCEAN

SOUTH
AMERICA

A ●

## 1 AYERS ROCK

Also known as Uluru, this large rock stands in the Australian outback today. How did it form?

a. from sand compacted at the bottom of an ancient sea
b. in a volcanic eruption
c. after an earthquake
d. by being carved out by rain and rivers

## 2 CAVE OF CRYSTALS

Why is it dangerous for people to go into this cave full of giant crystals at Naica in Mexico?

a. There are poisonous spiders.
b. There is no gravity.
c. It is extremely hot.
d. Crystals break and fall.

## 3 UYUNI SALT FLAT

In addition to salt, this vast, flat expanse—Salar de Uyuni in Bolivia—contains lots of lithium. What is lithium used to make?

a. oil
b. batteries
c. telescopes
d. breakfast cereal

ARCTIC OCEAN

EUROPE

ASIA

C

B

PACIFIC OCEAN

AFRICA

INDIAN OCEAN

E

ANTARCTICA

### 4 COTTON PALACE

Which ancient culture built a spa city called Hierapolis around these natural pools at Pamukkale, Turkey?

a. Chinese
b. Egyptian
c. Maya
d. Roman

### 5 RED BEACH

What turns a bright red color every fall on this beach in Panjin, China?

a. seaweed          c. rocks
b. tiny crabs       d. flowers

### 6 THE WAVE

What is this multicolored natural formation in Arizona, U.S.A., made out of?

a. glass            c. sandstone
b. spiderwebs       d. sugar

### 7–12

MATCH EACH OF THESE ATTRACTIONS TO THE RED DOT THAT SHOWS ITS LOCATION ON THE MAP.

CHECK YOUR ANSWERS ON PAGES 162–163.

# Life Zones

**1** POLAR BEARS LIVE IN ANTARCTICA.

**2** SEE-THROUGH CREATURES ARE COMMON IN THE OPEN OCEAN.

**3** ALASKA IS A GREAT PLACE TO GROW GIGANTIC VEGETABLES.

**4** ZEBRAS AND OSTRICHES OFTEN GRAZE TOGETHER IN AFRICA.

**5** WHITE FLAMINGOS ARE EXTREMELY RARE.

**6** CATTLE EGRETS EAT COWS.

**7** CLOWNFISH ARE RESISTANT TO THE DANGEROUS STING OF SEA ANEMONE TENTACLES.

**8** SAGEBRUSH IS COMMONLY FOUND IN PINE FORESTS.

**9** A VIRUS IS A LIVING CREATURE.

**10** MILLIONS OF YEARS AGO, PALM TREES GREW IN ANTARCTICA.

**11** PILOT FISH OFTEN SWIM ALONGSIDE SHARKS.

**12** THE ANACONDA LIVES IN THE DESERT.

**13** THE GROUND BELOW THE SURFACE OF THE TUNDRA IS PERMANENTLY FROZEN.

**14** CATTAILS GROW BEST IN OCEAN WATER.

**15** CORAL POLYPS GET FOOD FROM A PLANT GROWING INSIDE THEIR BODIES.

**16** A GROUP OF QUAKING ASPEN TREES WILL ALL CHANGE COLOR AT THE EXACT SAME TIME IN THE FALL.

**17** CARIBOU LIVE IN SOUTH AMERICA.

**18** A PARASITE LIVES ON OR IN ANOTHER LIVING THING.

**19** JACKALS AND COYOTES OFTEN COMPETE FOR PREY.

**20** GROVES OF MANGROVE TREES HELP PROTECT COASTLINES WHEN CYCLONES HIT.

**21** IN A SYMBIOTIC RELATIONSHIP, TWO CREATURES FIGHT EACH OTHER FOR SURVIVAL.

**22** WILD LOBSTERS ONLY LIVE IN THE NORTHERN ATLANTIC OCEAN.

**23** NOTHING CAN SURVIVE AT THE BOTTOM OF THE MARIANA TRENCH, THE DEEPEST PLACE ON EARTH.

**24** MOSS IN ANTARCTICA FEEDS ON PENGUIN POOP.

**25** THE GOBI, A DESERT IN CENTRAL ASIA, IS ONE OF THE BEST PLACES TO HUNT FOR FOSSILS.

**26** TREES GROW AT THE SUMMIT OF MOUNT EVEREST.

**27** SHARKS LIKE TO CHOMP ON LIVE ELECTRIC CABLES AT THE BOTTOM OF THE OCEAN.

**28** DOLPHINS LIVE IN THE AMAZON RIVER.

**29** A COMMUNITY OF MANY DIFFERENT BACTERIA LIVE IN YOUR GUT.

**30** KANGAROOS HUNT AND EAT KOALAS.

CHECK YOUR ANSWERS ON PAGES 162–163.

# The Sandy SAHARA

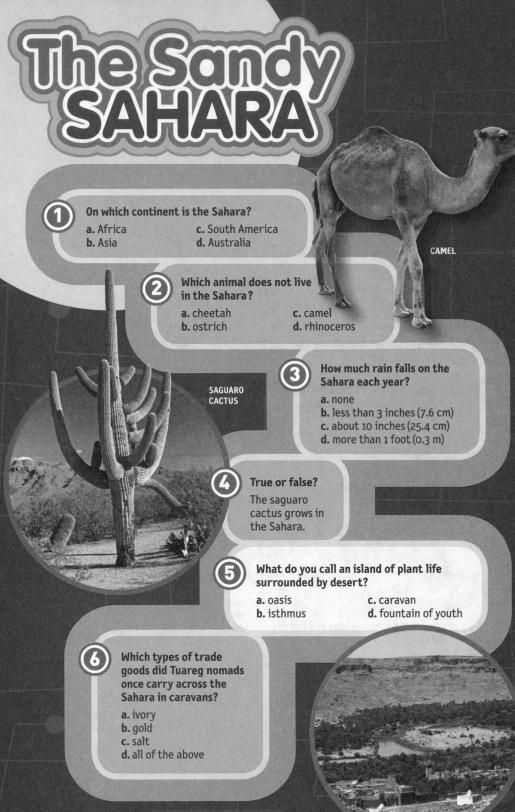

**1** On which continent is the Sahara?
a. Africa
b. Asia
c. South America
d. Australia

CAMEL

**2** Which animal does not live in the Sahara?
a. cheetah
b. ostrich
c. camel
d. rhinoceros

**3** How much rain falls on the Sahara each year?
a. none
b. less than 3 inches (7.6 cm)
c. about 10 inches (25.4 cm)
d. more than 1 foot (0.3 m)

SAGUARO CACTUS

**4** True or false?
The saguaro cactus grows in the Sahara.

**5** What do you call an island of plant life surrounded by desert?
a. oasis
b. isthmus
c. caravan
d. fountain of youth

**6** Which types of trade goods did Tuareg nomads once carry across the Sahara in caravans?
a. ivory
b. gold
c. salt
d. all of the above

DESERT ISLAND OF PLANTS

**7** What is an erg?
a. a desert turtle
b. an ancient egg
c. an area of shifting sand dunes
d. a superpowerful laser beam

**8** This Saharan resident is called a fennec. What is its closest relative?
a. rabbit      c. mongoose
b. lion        d. fox

FENNEC

**9** True or false?
The country of Niger established a large nature reserve in the Sahara.

**10** Which country is about the same size as the entire Sahara?
a. United States
b. Spain
c. Japan
d. India

**11** Blowing sand can create which shape in sand dunes?
a. a cube
b. a palm tree
c. a star
d. a sphere

**12** True or false?
Camels have two rows of long eyelashes.

SAND DUNES

# ULTIMATE NATURE CHALLENGE

**1** **TRUE OR FALSE?**

Goats can safely eat poison ivy.

**2** Which bird lives in the Sahara?
a. bald eagle
b. stork
c. ostrich
d. puffin

**3** Carlsbad Caverns in New Mexico, U.S.A., is home to what structure?
a. an ancient coral reef
b. a pyramid
c. termite mounds
d. the world's largest bee's nest

**4** **TRUE OR FALSE?**

In some parts of the Atacama Desert in Chile, it hasn't rained for 400 years.

**5** Which U.S. state is not on the Mississippi River's route?
a. Louisiana
b. Illinois
c. Tennessee
d. Nevada

**6** These green blobs from deserts in southern Africa are called living stones. What are they?
a. plants
b. snails
c. mushrooms
d. zebra poop

**7** If someone tells you a nor'easter is coming, what should you look out for?
a. a tidal wave
b. heavy snow and wind
c. a sandstorm
d. a cloud of locusts

⑧ **TRUE OR FALSE?**

No one has ever seen a pink grasshopper.

⑨ **Which flower is the first to bloom in the spring?**

a. tulip          c. lily

b. rose           d. daffodil

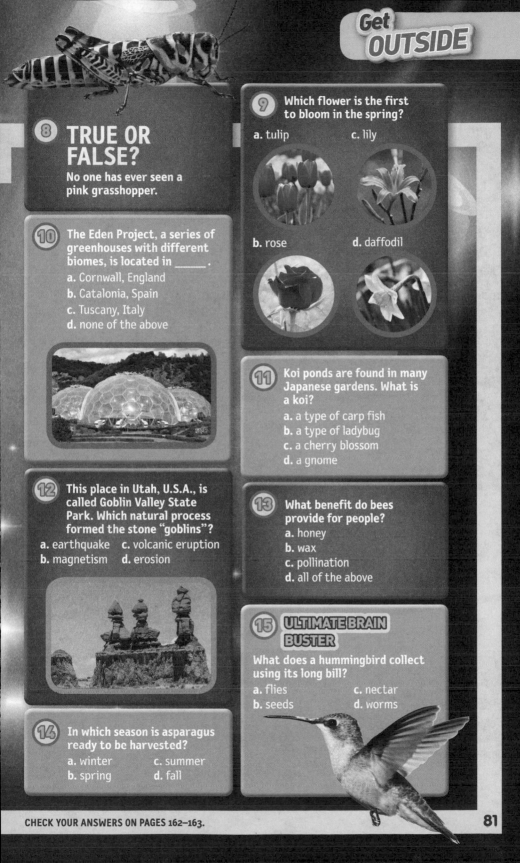

⑩ The Eden Project, a series of greenhouses with different biomes, is located in _____.
a. Cornwall, England
b. Catalonia, Spain
c. Tuscany, Italy
d. none of the above

⑪ Koi ponds are found in many Japanese gardens. What is a koi?
a. a type of carp fish
b. a type of ladybug
c. a cherry blossom
d. a gnome

⑫ This place in Utah, U.S.A., is called Goblin Valley State Park. Which natural process formed the stone "goblins"?
a. earthquake    c. volcanic eruption
b. magnetism     d. erosion

⑬ What benefit do bees provide for people?
a. honey
b. wax
c. pollination
d. all of the above

⑮ **ULTIMATE BRAIN BUSTER**

What does a hummingbird collect using its long bill?
a. flies          c. nectar
b. seeds          d. worms

⑭ In which season is asparagus ready to be harvested?
a. winter         c. summer
b. spring         d. fall

CHECK YOUR ANSWERS ON PAGES 162–163.

ARCHAEOLOGISTS AT WORK IN THE RUINS OF POMPEII, ITALY

82

# IT'S GREEK TO ME

**1** The Parthenon—pictured here—was built to honor which **Greek** god?

a. Poseidon    c. Hera
b. Athena    d. Zeus

**2** True or false? From about 750 to 500 B.C., male citizens wore **togas** made of wool.

**3** Who was *not* a **Greek** philosopher?

a. Socrates    c. Cicero
b. Aristotle    d. Plato

**4** **Pegasus** was a mythological creature that looked like a horse with _____.

a. wings
b. the torso of a man
c. a snake's head
d. the rear end of a lion

**5** True or false? The Greeks developed the **first** alphabet.

**6** The **Olympics,** which began about 2,790 years ago, gets its name from _____.

a. the Greek word for "champions"
b. the Greek town of Olympia, where they were first held
c. the god Olympus, as athletes were viewed as gods of Earth
d. the Emperor Olympus, who ruled Greece at the time

**7** What was the name of the **silver** coins used for money in ancient Greece?

a. drachmas    c. lire
b. aureus    d. euros

**8** According to Greek myth, Hades tricked Persephone into eating the seeds of which **fruit** to make her return to the underworld each year?

a. apple
b. kiwi
c. orange
d. pomegranate

THE PARTHENON IN ATHENS, GREECE

**9** Euclid, a **Greek** mathematician, is considered the father of which math subject?

a. algebra
b. geometry
c. calculus
d. computer programming

**10** The **ancient** Greeks believed in government run by all citizens, leading to the modern system of ____.

a. monarchy
b. dictatorship
c. voting booths
d. democracy

**11** Who **wrote** the epic poems the *Iliad* and the *Odyssey*, which describe the Trojan War and the travels of Odysseus after the fall of Troy?

a. Euripides
b. Homer
c. Sophocles
d. Hera

**12** True or false? Ancient Greeks used olive oil to **wash** their faces.

CHECK YOUR ANSWERS ON PAGES 164–165.

# History's Headlines

1  OCTOBER 29, 1929: WALL STREET STOCK MARKET CRASHES ON BLACK FRIDAY.

2  MARCH 15, 44 B.C.: JULIUS CAESAR IS ASSASSINATED BY POLITICAL RIVALS.

3  OCTOBER 4, 1957: RUSSIA LAUNCHES THE FIRST SATELLITE, SPUTNIK 1, INTO SPACE.

4  APRIL 15, 1947: JACKIE ROBINSON BECOMES THE FIRST AFRICAN-AMERICAN BASEBALL PLAYER IN MAJOR LEAGUE BASEBALL.

5  1347: THE BLACK DEATH PLAGUE HITS ROME, ITALY.

6  JANUARY 1, 1863: PRESIDENT ABRAHAM LINCOLN'S EMANCIPATION PROCLAMATION ENDS THE U.S. CIVIL WAR.

7  APRIL 15, 1912: BRITAIN'S "UNSINKABLE" SHIP, THE R.M.S. *TITANIC*, SINKS AFTER HITTING AN ICEBERG. THERE ARE NO SURVIVORS.

8  1512: LEONARDO DA VINCI FINISHES PAINTING THE CEILING OF THE SISTINE CHAPEL.

9  NOVEMBER 9, 1989: THE BERLIN WALL COMES DOWN, REUNITING NORTH AND SOUTH GERMANY.

10  1332 B.C.: THE "BOY KING" TUTANKHAMUN IS MADE PHARAOH AT AGE SIX.

11  NOVEMBER 6, 1893: GEORGE FERRIS'S BIG WHEEL IS A BIG HIT AT THE CHICAGO WORLD'S FAIR.

12  1454: JOHANNES GUTENBERG USES THE PRINTING PRESS FOR THE FIRST TIME TO MASS-PRODUCE A BOOK OF FAIRY TALES.

13  JUNE 28, 1914: ARCHDUKE FERDINAND OF AUSTRIA IS ASSASSINATED, STARTING WORLD WAR I.

14  JULY 20, 1969: NASA ASTRONAUT NEIL ARMSTRONG TAKES HUMANKIND'S FIRST STEPS ON THE MOON.

15  AUGUST, A.D. 79: AN EARTHQUAKE HITS ITALY, DESTROYING THE TOWN OF POMPEII.

**16** SEPTEMBER 11, 2001: TERRORISTS CRASH PLANES INTO THE WORLD TRADE CENTER IN NEW YORK CITY, U.S.A.

**17** OCTOBER 12, 1492: CHRISTOPHER COLUMBUS REACHES THE NEW WORLD AFTER SIX MONTHS AT SEA.

**18** OCTOBER 1, 1949: MAO ZEDONG ESTABLISHES DEMOCRACY IN CHINA.

**19** AUGUST 28, 1963: DR. MARTIN LUTHER KING, JR., DELIVERS HIS "I HAVE A DREAM" SPEECH IN LOS ANGELES, CALIFORNIA, U.S.A.

**20** AUGUST 6, 1945: THE UNITED STATES DROPS AN ATOMIC BOMB ON HIROSHIMA, JAPAN.

**21** 2,000,000 B.C.: EARLY HUMAN ANCESTOR *HOMO ERECTUS* BEGINS USING TOOLS IN AFRICA.

**22** NOVEMBER 22, 1963: PRESIDENT JOHN F. KENNEDY AND HIS WIFE JACQUELINE ARE ASSASSINATED IN DALLAS, TEXAS, U.S.A.

**23** 1450: THE INCA BEGIN WORK ON THE CITY OF MACHU PICCHU, WHICH IS NESTLED HIGH IN THE ANDES.

**24** AUGUST 24, 2006: PLUTO GETS DEMOTED TO A DWARF PLANET.

**25** 1221: GENGHIS KHAN CONQUERS KHWARIZM EMPIRE, CONNECTING CHINA AND EUROPE.

**26** DECEMBER 17, 1903: THE WRIGHT BROTHERS TAKE THE FIRST FLIGHT, IN KITTY HAWK, NORTH CAROLINA, U.S.A.

**27** JUNE 17, 1991: PRESIDENT NELSON MANDELA'S GOVERNMENT ENDS APARTHEID IN SOUTH AFRICA.

**28** 1972: NINTENDO ODYSSEY, THE FIRST HOME VIDEO GAME SYSTEM, HITS STORE SHELVES.

**29** 1453: OTTOMANS CONQUER CONSTANTINOPLE, THE CAPITAL OF THE BYZANTINE EMPIRE.

**30** MAY 29, 1953: SIR EDMUND HILLARY OF THE U.K. AND SHERPA TENZIG NORGAY OF NEPAL ARE THE FIRST CLIMBERS TO REACH THE SUMMIT OF MOUNT EVEREST.

CHECK YOUR ANSWERS ON PAGES 164–165.

# MAP MANIA!
# DIG THIS!

**A**ncient people and cultures left behind many objects that archaeologists have uncovered. These objects reveal what life was like long ago.

NORTH AMERICA

D

E

ATLANTIC OCEAN

PACIFIC OCEAN

SOUTH AMERICA

C

## 1 NASCA, PERU

Giant pictures—like this one of a bird—carved into the desert by the Nasca people about 2,000 years ago are called _____.

a. geoglyphs
b. earthlines
c. geometric ridges
d. sky doodles

## 2 LEICESTER, U.K.

Where were the remains of King Richard III, who was the last English king to die on the battlefield, found in 2012?

a. under Buckingham Palace
b. in a secret tomb
c. under a parking lot
d. in a garbage dump

## 3 XI'AN, CHINA

Emperor Qin was buried in his tomb with a terra-cotta army to protect him in the afterlife. What are the life-size statues made of?

a. bronze
b. clay
c. wood
d. gold

### 4. MESA VERDE NATIONAL PARK, U.S.A.

The Anasazi people built their homes into cliffs. Which modern-day Native American people are the descendants of the Anasazi?

a. Lenape
c. Eskimo
b. Pueblo
d. Cherokee

ARCTIC OCEAN

EUROPE

ASIA

A

AFRICA

B

F

PACIFIC OCEAN

INDIAN OCEAN

AUSTRALIA

ANTARCTICA

ARTIST'S IMPRESSION OF ARDI

### 5. AFAR DESERT, ETHIOPIA

In 2009, the oldest fossil of a human ancestor was found and named Ardi. About how old is this fossil?

a. 1.2 million years
c. 3.2 million years
b. 2.8 million years
d. 4.4 million years

### 6. ROSETTA, EGYPT

The Rosetta Stone is a key to translating hieroglyphics into which language?

a. Greek
c. cuneiform
b. French
d. Pig Latin

### 7–12

MATCH EACH OF THESE SIX ARCHAEOLOGICAL FINDS TO THE RED DOT ON THE MAP THAT SHOWS ITS LOCATION.

# Show STOPPERS

**1** Trick horse rider Philip Astley opened Astley's Amphitheater in 1773 and is considered the father of the modern circus. Where was the theater located?

a. Paris, France
b. Philadelphia, U.S.A.
c. London, England
d. Edinburgh, Scotland

CIRCUS HORSE RIDERS

**2** The _____ Wallendas are a family of circus performers and acrobats who have entertained crowds since about 1780.

a. Flying
b. Wily
c. Well-balanced
d. Fearless

**3** True or false?
In ancient Rome, all gladiators were male.

ROMAN GLADIATOR RE-ENACTORS

**4** In 2012 the Steel Pier in Atlantic City, New Jersey, U.S.A., announced plans to revive which popular act from the 1920s?

a. the Diving Horse
b. the Bearded Lady
c. the Cannonball Man
d. the Clown Car

**5** French acrobat Jules Léotard was the first person to ever perform which circus act in 1859?

a. lion taming
b. tightrope walking
c. fire breathing
d. flying trapeze

**6** Performers of *corde lisse* put on what type of acrobatic circus act?

**a.** rope climbing  **c.** trampoline jumping
**b.** tightrope walking  **d.** contortionism

**7** **True or false?**
The earliest records of juggling come from ancient Greece.

**8** What were the traveling singers and entertainers of the Middle Ages called?

**a.** minstrels  **c.** jongleurs
**b.** troubadours  **d.** all of the above

**9** What U.S. Civil War soldier eventually became the star of his own Wild West show?

**a.** Davy Crockett
**b.** Will Rogers
**c.** "Buffalo" Bill Cody
**d.** Daniel Boone

TRAVELING MUSICIAN ARTWORK

**10** Which touring circus has been in operation since 1888, making it the world's oldest?

**a.** Ringling Bros. and Barnum & Bailey Circus, U.S.A.
**b.** Circo Atayde, Mexico
**c.** Cirque du Soleil, Canada
**d.** Pinders Circus, U.K.

**11** **True or false?**
Several Olympians are acrobats for Cirque du Soleil.

**12** What is the term for fear of clowns?

**a.** coulrophobia
**b.** trichopathophobia
**c.** cherophobia
**d.** bozophobia

CIRQUE DU SOLEIL

# GIRL POWER

**1** How old was Queen Elizabeth I when she became **ruler** of England?

a. 19
b. 25
c. 33
d. 38

**2** True or false? Sacagawea brought her infant **son** along on Lewis and Clark's 1804–1806 expedition to the American West.

CORONATION PORTRAIT OF ELIZABETH I

**3** Frida Kahlo was a Mexican artist and **feminist** who survived both polio and a terrible bus accident. What type of art did she make?

a. self-portraits
b. sculptures
c. abstract drawings
d. woodcut prints

**4** In 1963, who became the first **woman** to travel into space?

a. Sally Ride, U.S.A.
b. Valentina Tereshkova, Russia
c. Helen Sharman, U.K.
d. Svetlana Savitskaya, Russia

**5** In 1966, Indira Ghandi became which country's first female **leader** and prime minister?

a. Russia          c. Nigeria
b. Singapore       d. India

**6** True or false? Marie Curie became the first **woman** to win a Nobel Prize.

**7** Who was the first woman on the U.S. Supreme Court?

a. Sandra Day O'Connor
b. Ruth Bader Ginsburg
c. Sonia Sotomayor
d. Hillary Clinton

**8** What did **French** fashion designer and style icon Gabrielle "Coco" Chanel do before she opened her first shop in 1910?

a. worked at a bank
b. made perfume
c. performed a trapeze act
d. sang in music clubs

**9** In **2012**, a Pakistani girl named Malala Yousafzai was attacked because she had spoken out in support of her right to _____.

a. health care     c. wear pink
b. an education    d. all of the above

**10** In 1849, which female medical professional was the first American woman to earn a medical **degree?**

a. Elizabeth Blackwell    c. Florence Nightingale
b. Clara Barton           d. Dorothea Dix

**11** True or false? In 1428, Joan of Arc led the French Army to **victory** at the Battle of Toulouse.

**12** In the 500s, which empress fought for laws for women's rights in her realm?

a. Wu Zetian, China    c. Suiko, Japan
b. Lucilla, Rome       d. Theodora, Byzantine

# THE SECRETS OF EASTER ISLAND

**1** Easter Island, also called Rapa Nui, is located in the South Pacific Ocean and is one of the most remote islands in the world. It is a special territory of which country?

a. Australia
b. Papua New Guinea
c. Bali
d. Chile

**2** The most famous sight on Easter Island are these giant statues called moai. How many moai have been found so far?

a. 233
b. 545
c. 778
d. 887

**3** True or false?
The moai are just giant heads; they have no torsos or legs.

**4** The moai are carved out of _____ .

a. compressed volcanic ash
b. sandstone
c. seashells glued together
d. black marble

**5** When do scientists think the first Polynesian settlers traveling in canoes and catamarans arrived on Easter Island?

a. 100 B.C.
b. A.D. 200
c. A.D. 500
d. A.D. 800

**6** In 1722, Dutch explorers were the first Europeans to visit the island. They named it Easter Island because _____.

a. they arrived on Easter Sunday
b. the moai looked like the Easter Bunny
c. it was east of the last island they visited
d. their boat was named *Easter*

MOAI AT RANO RARAKU
QUARRY ON EASTER ISLAND

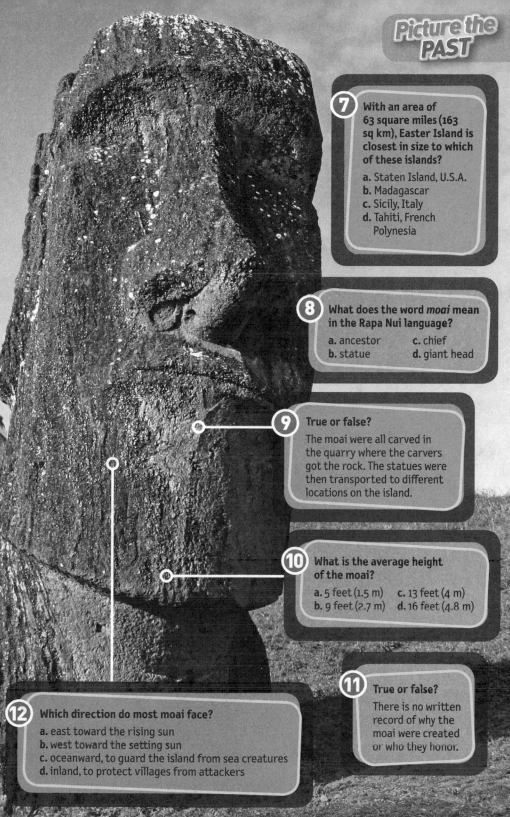

**7** With an area of 63 square miles (163 sq km), Easter Island is closest in size to which of these islands?

a. Staten Island, U.S.A.
b. Madagascar
c. Sicily, Italy
d. Tahiti, French Polynesia

**8** What does the word *moai* mean in the Rapa Nui language?

a. ancestor    c. chief
b. statue    d. giant head

**9** True or false?
The moai were all carved in the quarry where the carvers got the rock. The statues were then transported to different locations on the island.

**10** What is the average height of the moai?

a. 5 feet (1.5 m)    c. 13 feet (4 m)
b. 9 feet (2.7 m)    d. 16 feet (4.8 m)

**11** True or false?
There is no written record of why the moai were created or who they honor.

**12** Which direction do most moai face?

a. east toward the rising sun
b. west toward the setting sun
c. oceanward, to guard the island from sea creatures
d. inland, to protect villages from attackers

# The Royal TREATMENT

JULIUS CAESAR

**1** Which country did William the Conqueror (1028–1087) take over?
a. England
b. France
c. Norway
d. Italy

WILLIAM THE CONQUEROR

**2** Julius Caesar became leader of which ancient empire?
a. Roman
b. Greek
c. Persian
d. French

**3** Which country does not currently have a royal family?
a. Saudi Arabia
b. Russia
c. Thailand
d. Spain

**4** Where are the British crown jewels kept?
a. in the queen's sock drawer
b. Buckingham Palace
c. Big Ben
d. Tower of London

**5** Which of the following is not a title for a monarch?
a. King
b. Emperor
c. Regent
d. Sultan

**6** Albert III of Austria, who ruled from 1365 to 1395, was known as "Albert with the _____," because he wore a lock of his wife's hair in this hairstyle.
a. Mohawk
b. Pigtail
c. French Braid
d. Rat-tail

BRITISH CROWN JEWELS

**7** True or false?
Alexander the Great named a city he conquered after his beloved horse Bucephalus.

ALEXANDER THE GREAT

**8** King Goodwill Zwelithini is the leader of the Zulu people, the largest tribe in which African country?
**a.** South Africa    **c.** Cameroon
**b.** Ghana    **d.** Ethiopia

**9** Rising to power in 1867 at age 14, Emperor Meiji unified which country and ushered it into the modern era?
**a.** China    **c.** India
**b.** Turkey    **d.** Japan

**10** Ivan the Terrible was the grandson of which other famously nicknamed Russian ruler?
**a.** Catherine the Great    **c.** Nicholas the Bloody
**b.** Alexander the Blessed    **d.** Ivan the Great

**11** The Forbidden City is the Chinese Imperial Palace. It was built in the early 1400s during which dynasty?
**a.** Tang    **c.** Qing
**b.** Manchu    **d.** Ming

**12** Which British queen was known as the "Grandmother of Europe" because her grandchildren ruled Great Britain, Prussia, Greece, Romania, Russia, Norway, Sweden, and Spain?
**a.** Queen Victoria
**b.** Queen Elizabeth I
**c.** Queen Elizabeth II
**d.** Queen Anne

CHECK YOUR ANSWERS ON PAGES 164–165.

# BATTLE ZONES

**1** **Napoleon** Bonaparte was finally defeated at the Battle of Waterloo on June 18, 1815. In which modern-day country is Waterloo?

a. France
b. Germany
c. Belgium
d. Russia

**2** With about 23,000 **Confederate** and Union soldiers dead, wounded, or missing, where was the bloodiest day of the U.S. Civil War fought?

a. Antietam, Maryland
b. Gettysburg, Pennsylvania
c. Shiloh, Tennessee
d. Vicksburg, Mississippi

**3** In 1953, the **Battle** of Dien Bien Phu freed Vietnam from the rule of which country?

a. England
b. France
c. China
d. Holland

**4** In 1781, which U.S. leader defeated the British Army at the Battle of Yorktown in the **American** Revolutionary War?

a. George Washington
b. Richard Montgomery
c. Benedict Arnold
d. Nathanael Greene

RE-ENACTMENT OF THE BATTLE OF WATERLOO, 1815

**5** True or false? Macedonian leader Alexander the Great (356–323 B.C.) never lost a **battle**.

**6** The **Allied** forces turned the tide of World War II with the D-Day invasion of France. What is the "D" believed to stand for?

a. defense          c. deliverance
b. decision         d. day

**7** A trebuchet was a type of _____ used to launch rocks in **sieges** during the Middle Ages.

a. siege tower      c. catapult
b. battering ram    d. giant sword

**8** In which U.S. city did soldiers defend the **Alamo** for 13 days before falling to Santa Anna's army during the Texas Revolution?

a. Houston          c. El Paso
b. Austin           d. San Antonio

**9** Francisco Pizarro led about 200 men to victory against 80,000 soldiers to defeat which empire in 1532?

a. Maya             c. Inca
b. Egyptian         d. Aztec

**10** What **color** flag traditionally indicates that an enemy wants to surrender?

a. black
b. white
c. red
d. blue

CHECK YOUR ANSWERS ON PAGES 164–165.

# GAME SHOW

# ULTIMATE HISTORY CHALLENGE

**1** In the original Greek Olympic Games, what did first-place winners win?

a. silver cups
b. a handshake from the emperor
c. wreaths made of olive tree branches
d. new chariots

**2** TRUE OR FALSE?

According to myth, the Greek gods lived under Mount Olympus.

**3** The Great Ziggurat of Ur was built by which ancient culture?

a. Maya          c. Sumerian
b. Inca          d. Roman

**4** In 2000, archaeologists diving in the Mediterranean Sea found a sunken city that was lost for 1,200 years near what modern-day city?

a. Alexandria, Egypt
b. Athens, Greece
c. Naples, Italy
d. Barcelona, Spain

**5** What is the name of the arena where Roman chariot races were held?

a. Circus Maximus
b. Hippodrome
c. Coliseum
d. Horsey Loop

**6** "Funambulism" is another word for which circus act?

a. tightrope walking
b. clowning
c. trapeze flying
d. contortionism

**7** Catherine the Great was which country's longest ruling female leader?

a. France    c. Finland
b. Spain    d. Russia

**8** In 2014, King Juan Carlos of Spain abdicated his throne. What does that mean?

a. He replaced it.
b. He retired, or stepped down.
c. He added a new back.
d. He removed the monarchy.

**9** TRUE OR FALSE?

Although many of her heroines get married at the end of her novels, Jane Austen herself never married.

**10** Some moai wear these red pukao on their heads. What do historians think they could be?

a. hats
b. headdresses
c. topknot hairstyles
d. all of the above

**11** The Battle of Stalingrad, a turning point in World War II, was one of the bloodiest battles in history. About how many casualties were there?

a. 1 million    c. 2 million
b. 1.5 million    d. 3.5 million

**12** Which medical organization did pioneering nurse Clara Barton found?

a. The Red Cross
b. The National Institutes of Health
c. Doctors Without Borders
d. Centers for Disease Control

**13** The army from which empire brought 15 war elephants to fight Alexander the Great at the Battle of Gaugamela in 331 B.C.?

a. Persian    c. Ottoman
b. Greek    d. Mongolian

**14** ULTIMATE BRAIN BUSTER

TRUE OR FALSE?

There were no human casualties at the Battle of Fort Sumter, which was the first battle of the U.S. Civil War.

THE START OF A HORSE RACE

# It's a Numbers GAME

**1.** Thirty-two soccer teams played in the World Cup championship in Brazil in 2014. The total number of games played was _____.

a. 16
b. 32
c. 64
d. 2,014

WORLD CUP SOCCER PLAYER

**2.** In 2014, Lucy Li became the youngest golfer ever to compete in the U.S. Women's Open. How old was she?

a. 6
b. 11
c. 15
d. 38

**3.** Mancala is considered the world's oldest board game. Players move pebbles from cup to cup. How many cups are there?

a. 8
b. 14
c. 18
d. 24

**4.** The height of a racehorse is usually 15 to 17 hands tall. A hand is _____ high.

a. 2 inches (5.1 cm)
b. 4 inches (10.2 cm)
c. 1 foot (30.5 cm)
d. 1 hoof

**5.** True or false?
On March 2, 1962, Wilt Chamberlain set the single-game NBA record by scoring 100 points.

**6.** Which of these board games was invented first? It was in 1888.

a. Monopoly
b. Tiddlywinks
c. Scrabble
d. Candyland

WILT CHAMBERLAIN

**7** When Mireia Belmonte Garcia of Spain finished the 1,500-meter freestyle swim in 15 minutes, 26.95 seconds on November 29, 2013, what was extra special about it?

a. It was her birthday.
b. Her teammates won every other race.
c. It was her third world record at the meet.
d. It occurred at 12:15 (and 26 seconds) p.m.

**8** **True or false?**

In 2008, at a height of 7 feet (2.1 m), Nikolay Valuev of Russia became the world's tallest skiing champion.

MIREIA BELMONTE
GARCIA

**9** What baseball record did Joe DiMaggio set in 1941 that still stands today?

a. most games in a row with a hit (56)
b. most home runs in a season (73)
c. most games played in a row (2,632)
d. most hot dogs eaten in one game (17)

**10** On July 30, 2014, Sabine Lisicki of Germany set the record for fastest women's tennis serve. Its speed was _____ .

a. 1.31 miles an hour (2.1 km/h)
b. 13.1 miles an hour (21.1 km/h)
c. 131 miles an hour (211 km/h)
d. 1,310 miles an hour (2,108 km/h)

ICE HOCKEY
PLAYER

**11** NFL yard lines are 10 yards (9.1 m) apart, but how tall are the numbers that label each line?

a. 6 inches (15.2 cm)
b. 6 feet (1.8 m)
c. 6 yards (5.5 m)
d. 6 miles (9.7 km)

**12** **True or false?**

Ice hockey is the only sport with games split into three periods.

INDIANAPOLIS 500

**13** How many times does a race car driver have to lap around the track to complete the Indianapolis 500 auto race in Indiana, U.S.A.?

a. 500
b. 200
c. 10
d. 1

# TAJ MAHAL

**2** **About how many years did it take to complete the Taj Mahal?**

a. 3 years        c. 50 years
b. 21 years       d. 100 years

**1** **Emperor Shah Jahan ordered construction of India's Taj Mahal in memory of his wife. Construction began in about the year ____ .**

a. 220 b.c.       c. 1908
b. 1632           d. 2011

**3** **There is a famous marble room below the dome with an interesting shape. How many walls does it have?**

a. 1, which is circular     c. 8
b. 4                        d. 27

**4** **True or false? About 1,000 elephants were used to transport materials during the Taj Mahal's construction.**

TAJ MAHAL

**6** **Workers from India, Persia, Europe, and the Ottoman Empire helped build the Taj Mahal. About how many people were there?**

a. 100            c. 20,000
b. 1,000          d. 100,000

**5** **About how much did it cost to build the Taj Mahal at the time?**

a. $68,000        c. $1,000,000
b. $279,000       d. $1,000,000,000

**7** How much **land** around the Taj Mahal does India's government make sure stays clean?

a. 1 square mile (2.6 sq km)
b. 5 square miles (12.9 sq km)
c. 4,015 square miles (10,399 sq km)
d. 1 city block

**8** True or false? The Taj Mahal is open six days per week. It's closed on **Sundays.**

**9** Approximately how many people visit the Taj Mahal every year?

a. 500,000
b. 1 million
c. 3 million
d. 80 million

**10** Citizens of India pay 20 rupees to visit the Taj Mahal. How much do most tourists from other countries have to **pay**?

a. 750 rupees
b. 100 rupees
c. 25 rupees
d. 15 rupees

**11** How tall is the Taj Mahal's **central** dome?

a. 50 feet (15 m)
b. 240 feet (73 m)
c. 510 feet (155 m)
d. 1,000 feet (305 m)

**13** True or false? When a sound is made inside the **tomb** at the Taj Mahal, it takes 28 seconds until the echoes produced by the sound end.

**12** How **tall** are the towers on the four corners of the Taj Mahal?

a. 8 feet (2.4 m)
b. 25 feet (7.6 m)
c. 130 feet (39.6 m)
d. 310 feet (94.5 m)

CHECK YOUR ANSWERS ON PAGES 165–166.

# Pay DAY!

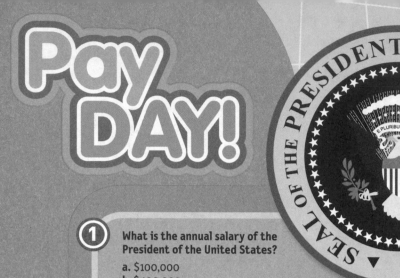

PRESIDENTIAL SEAL

**1** What is the annual salary of the President of the United States?

a. $100,000
b. $400,000
c. $1,000,000
d. one of each coin and bill with a president's face on it

**2** What is the average salary for a computer programmer in the United States?

a. $43,200
b. $65,400
c. $71,300
d. $84,900

**3** For 2014, the world's highest paid athlete in a team sport was soccer star Cristiano Ronaldo. How much did he earn?

a. $50,000,000
b. $80,000,000
c. $100,000,000
d. $5 a game

**4** True or false?

The world's top paid athlete in 2014, earning $105,000,000, was tennis star Roger Federer.

**5** In 2014, $96,635 was the highest average amount earned per person in which country?

a. Qatar
b. United States
c. Japan
d. Canada

ROGER FEDERER

CHECK YOUR ANSWERS ON PAGES 165–166.

**6** **True or false?**
In 1927, Babe Ruth became the first athlete to sign a million-dollar-a-year contract.

**7** In 2014, the city with the most billionaires in the world—72—was_____.
a. New York, New York, U.S.A.
b. Moscow, Russia
c. London, England
d. Hong Kong, China

**8** This item, which makes up about 3.5 percent of the oceans, is where we get the word "salary" from.
a. salt
b. shells
c. sand
d. seaweed

**9** As of 2014, heads of Apple, Facebook, Google, and other technology companies all receive the same salary of _____.
a. $1 a year
b. $1 million a year
c. $1 billion a year
d. $1 trillion a year

**10** **True or false?**
Having earned about $75 million in a year, Robert Downey, Jr., who plays Iron Man, was named Hollywood's highest paid actor for 2014.

IRON MAN

# MAP MANIA!
# HOW MANY PEOPLE?

**T**est your knowledge of different facts about the human population.

ATLANTIC OCEAN

NORTH AMERICA

PACIFIC OCEAN

SOUTH AMERICA

B

E

## 1 INDIA

India and China both have populations made up of _____.

**a.** more than 1 billion people
**b.** more than 1 million people
**c.** a split of 50 percent men, 50 percent women
**d.** people who are smiling right now

## 2 VATICAN CITY

Only about 800 people live in this tiny country, located inside Rome, Italy. Who is one of those people?

**a.** the president of Italy
**b.** the head of the United Nations
**c.** the pope (leader of the Roman Catholic Church)
**d.** Michael Jordan

## 3 SOUTH AFRICA

With a population of about 53 million people, South Africa has more official languages than any other country. How many does it have?

**a.** 4          **c.** 260
**b.** 11         **d.** 44 million

# Go FIGURE!

## 4 ICELAND

With a population of about 323,000, Iceland has the world's highest percentage of people with Internet access. What is that percentage?

a. 52
b. 71.5
c. 96.5
d. 100

**ARCTIC OCEAN**

EUROPE

**F**

ASIA

AFRICA

**C**

PACIFIC OCEAN

INDIAN OCEAN

**D**

AUSTRALIA

**A**

## 5 INCA EMPIRE

The Inca Empire rose to power in the 15th and 16th centuries in what is now Peru. What was the empire's population at its peak?

a. about 12,000,000
b. about 12,000
c. 1,200
d. 12

## 6 ANTARCTICA

No people live in Antarctica permanently, but about 5,000 scientists work there in the summer. About how many emperor penguins live in Antarctica?

a. 600
b. 600,000
c. 6,000,000
d. 1 lonely penguin

## 7–12

MATCH EACH OF THESE REGIONS WITH THE LETTER ON THE MAP THAT MARKS ITS LOCATION.

# Go the DISTANCE

**1** What is the distance from Earth to the sun?
a. 9,296 miles (14,960 km)
b. 92,955,807 miles (149,597,870 km)
c. 92,960,000,000 miles (149,604,618,240 km)
d. 9 miles (14.5 km) but it's too hot—don't go

RUNNER

DIANA NYAD

**2** A running race that is 26.2 miles (42.2 km) long is known as a _____ .
a. sprint
b. olympiad
c. marathon
d. Pete

**3** In 2013, when 64-year-old Diana Nyad swam 103 miles (166 km), she became the first person to swim _____ .
a. from Cuba to Florida without a shark cage
b. 1,660 laps in a pool
c. more than 100 miles (161 km) with her eyes closed
d. more than 100 miles (161 km) in a gorilla suit

**4** True or false?
The longest manned balloon flight ever was two trips around the globe: 49,804 miles (80,152 km).

**5** The 2014 Tour de France bicycle race covered a total distance of _____ .
a. 2,277 miles (3,664 km)
b. 21 miles (33.8 km)
c. 2,100 feet (640 m)
d. 210 miles (336 km)

TOUR DE FRANCE

**6** Measuring 125,567 miles (202,081 km), the coastline of _____ is the longest in the world.

a. United States
b. Canada
c. Russia
d. Greenland

**7** In 2005, Nuno Gomes set the record for deepest dive with scuba gear. How far down did he go?

a. 104 feet (31.7 m)
b. 500 feet (152.4 m)
c. 1,044 feet (318.2 m)
d. to the bottom of a kiddie pool

**8** True or false?

An official international soccer field can be as short as 100 yards (91.4 m) and as long as 130 yards (118.9 m).

**9** A trip on the Trans-Siberian Railway in Russia covers 5,753 miles (9,259 km) from Moscow to Vladivostok and takes about _____ .

a. 3 hours
b. 1 week
c. 1 month
d. 1 year

BELLO NOCK

**10** When Niloofar Mosavar Rahmani of Sweden made a 531-foot (161.8-m) toss in 2010, she set a women's record. What did she throw?

a. Frisbee
b. shot-put
c. football
d. banana

**11** In 2010, American stuntman Bello Nock set the record for the longest tightrope walk without a safety device. How long was it?

a. 20 feet (6.1 m)
b. 113 feet (34.4 m)
c. 429 feet (130.8 m)
d. three baby steps

**12** True or false?

The farthest flight by a paper airplane has been 226 feet (68.9 m).

PAPER PLANE

# TRUE or FALSE?
# One to Thirty

**1** IN GREEK MYTHOLOGY, A CREATURE WITH ONE EYE IS KNOWN AS A CENTAUR.

**2** THERE IS A COMMON TYPE OF LADYBUG THAT HAS ONLY TWO SPOTS.

**3** IN THE LATE 1850S, THERE WAS A THREE-CENT COIN MINTED IN THE UNITED STATES.

**4** THE FOUR-O'CLOCK PLANT GETS ITS NAME BECAUSE IT OPENS UP VERY, VERY EARLY EACH DAY—AT ABOUT FOUR IN THE MORNING.

**5** FORMER BOXING GREAT GEORGE FOREMAN HAS FIVE SONS NAMED GEORGE.

**6** THE SIX-EYED SAND SPIDER IS FOUND ONLY IN ASIA.

**7** *SNOW WHITE AND THE SEVEN DWARFS* WAS THE FIRST FULL-LENGTH ANIMATED MOVIE.

**8** ANOTHER NAME FOR THE POPULAR POOL GAME 8-BALL IS MAGIC BALL.

**9** IN 2006, THE INTERNATIONAL ASTRONOMICAL UNION AGREED THAT OUR SOLAR SYSTEM HAS NINE PLANETS.

**10** OUR REGULAR SYSTEM FOR WRITING NUMBERS IS KNOWN AS "BASE-10."

**11** SEVEN-ELEVEN (7-11) STORES GOT THEIR NAME BECAUSE THE FOUNDER WAS BORN ON JULY 11.

**12** IN 2013, IT WAS DETERMINED THAT BUYING ALL THE ITEMS MENTIONED IN THE SONG "THE 12 DAYS OF CHRISTMAS" WOULD COST $27,393.17.

**13** ARITHMOPHOBIA IS THE FEAR OF THE NUMBER 13.

**14** THE BONNET IS A CERTAIN KIND OF POEM WITH 14 LINES.

**15** THE FIRST POINT IN A TENNIS GAME IS NOTED WITH THE NUMBER 15.

**16** IN CHESS, EACH PLAYER STARTS THE GAME WITH 16 PIECES.

**17** JUNE 17 IS NORWAY'S INDEPENDENCE DAY.

**18** ARGON IS THE 18TH ELEMENT IN THE PERIODIC TABLE OF ELEMENTS.

**19** THERE ARE 19 SEPARATE POPULATIONS OF POLAR BEARS IN THE ARCTIC.

**20** A DARTBOARD IS DIVIDED INTO 20 SECTIONS.

**21** CITIZENS OF KUWAIT HAVE TO BE AT LEAST 21 YEARS OLD TO VOTE.

**22** THERE ARE 22 LETTERS IN THE HEBREW ALPHABET.

**23** "23 SKIDOO" WAS A SLANG PHRASE IN THE UNITED STATES IN THE EARLY 20TH CENTURY. IT MEANT "COME HERE RIGHT NOW."

**24** THE ITALIANS CAME UP WITH THE 24-HOUR DAY, BASED ON WHEN 24 SPECIFIC STARS APPEARED IN THE SKY.

**25** A BOARD GAME CALLED PACHISI (FROM A WORD MEANING "25") HAS BEEN CALLED THE NATIONAL GAME OF INDIA.

**26** YOU HAVE 26 BONES IN EACH OF YOUR FEET.

**27** IN BASEBALL, IF A PITCHER GETS 27 OUTS WITHOUT ALLOWING A BATTER TO REACH BASE, IT'S CALLED A GRAND SLAM.

**28** IN A GAME OF DOMINOES, EACH PLAYER STARTS WITH 28 TILES.

**29** IT TAKES SATURN MORE THAN 29 YEARS TO ORBIT THE SUN.

**30** IN 2012, A COMPANY IN CHINA BUILT A 30-STORY HOTEL IN JUST 15 DAYS.

CHECK YOUR ANSWERS ON PAGES 165–166.

# OFF THE SCALE

**1** True or false? On the **Celsius** temperature scale, water freezes at 0° and boils at 100°.

**2** On the Fahrenheit scale, 32° is the freezing point of water. What is its **boiling** point?

a. 98.6°      c. 212°
b. 100°      d. 451°

**3** True or false? The Beaufort scale measures the **force** of wind on a scale of 1 to 100.

**4** The **Mohs scale** goes from 1 (softest) to 10 (hardest). It is used to measure _____.

a. minerals (diamonds, quartz, and so on)
b. eggshells (of different animals)
c. metals
d. pillows

**5** A scale based on the strength of the wind measures damage from tornados. What is this **scale** called?

a. funnel scale      c. Fujita scale
b. twister scale      d. bathroom scale

**6** The strength of earthquakes is measured using the "moment magnitude scale." With each increase of 1 on the scale, how much greater is the **intensity** of the quake?

a. 5 times      c. 100 times
b. 10 times      d. too shaky to read the answer

ICE IN A FROZEN RIVER

**7** The Saffir-Simpson scale measures **wind** from 1 to 5. But what type of winds is this scale measuring?

a. snow      c. desert
b. hurricane      d. fans

**8** True or false? Dividing a minute into 60 seconds and an hour into 60 minutes comes from a number system going back to **3500** B.C.

**9** What is the name of the scale from 0 to 16 million that is used to measure the spiciness of chili **peppers**?

a. Scoville      c. chili challenge
b. pepper points      d. please pass the water

**10** An entomologist named Justin Schmidt came up with a 1-to-4 scale measuring which type of **pain**?

a. dog bites      c. insect stings
b. frostbite      d. chemical burns

**11** The nanoscale measures incredibly small things. How **many** nanometers thick is a sheet of paper?

a. 1      c. 100,000
b. 100      d. 100,000,000

**12** True or false? In about 45 B.C., Julius Caesar introduced a **calendar** with **365** days.

CHECK YOUR ANSWERS ON PAGES 165–166.

# GAME SHOW
# ULTIMATE NUMBER CHALLENGE

**1** The surface of a soccer ball is made with _____ panels of leather.
a. 18          c. 32
b. 26          d. any of the above

**2** In 2007, more than 100 million people voted to include the Taj Mahal on what list?
a. New Seven Wonders of the World
b. 20th location for the *Big Brother* TV show
c. 50 Places to Visit in Your Lifetime
d. 2007 Building of the Year

**3** In 1963, how much was artist Harvey Ball paid to create the very famous image pictured here?
a. $45,000,000
b. $45
c. $4,500
d. 45¢

**4** TRUE OR FALSE?
It is predicted that in the year 2100 the pictured continent will contain 40 percent of the world's population.

**5** In 1988, Galina Chistyakova set the world record for women's long jump. How far did she jump?
a. 10 feet, 4 inches (3.1 m)
b. 13 feet, 6 inches (4.1 m)
c. 24 feet, 8 inches (7.5 m)
d. still waiting for her to land

**6** The term "karat" is used to describe the quality of _____ ?
a. diamonds     c. rubies
b. gold          d. carrots

**7** TRUE OR FALSE?
On a bottle of sunscreen, the SPF number (2 to 70) indicates how many minutes you can stay out before getting burned.

SUNCREAM
FACTOR 30

**8** On July 1, 1859, Amherst defeated Williams 73 to 32. It was the first _____ .
a. college basketball game
b. college baseball game
c. college football game
d. time players wore shoes while playing tennis

**9** TRUE OR FALSE?
Kellogg's cereal Product 19, introduced in 1967, got its name because it contained 19 vitamins and minerals.

**10** In 2011, the world population passed _____ for the first time.
a. 7 million      c. 7 trillion
b. 7 billion      d. 2,011

**11** TRUE OR FALSE?
In 2014, *The Hunger Games*'s Jennifer Lawrence was the highest paid actress, earning $51 million in 12 months.

**12** TRUE OR FALSE?
The land around the Taj Mahal is 84 acres (34 ha), about the same area as 64 football fields.

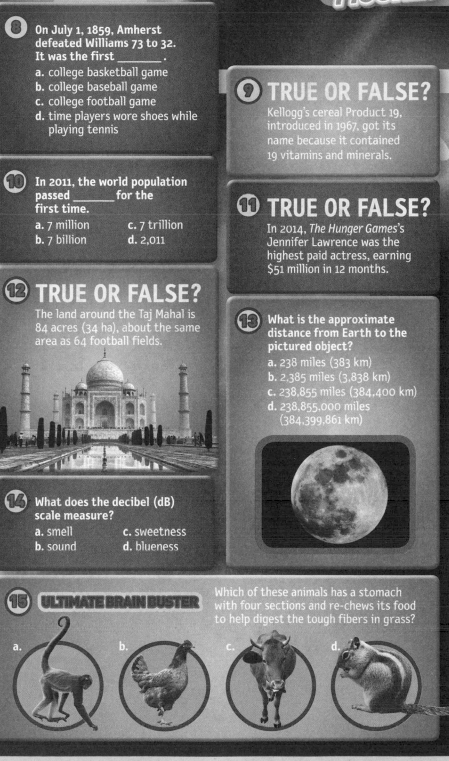

**13** What is the approximate distance from Earth to the pictured object?
a. 238 miles (383 km)
b. 2,385 miles (3,838 km)
c. 238,855 miles (384,400 km)
d. 238,855,000 miles (384,399,861 km)

**14** What does the decibel (dB) scale measure?
a. smell       c. sweetness
b. sound       d. blueness

**15** ULTIMATE BRAIN BUSTER
Which of these animals has a stomach with four sections and re-chews its food to help digest the tough fibers in grass?
a.
b.
c.
d.

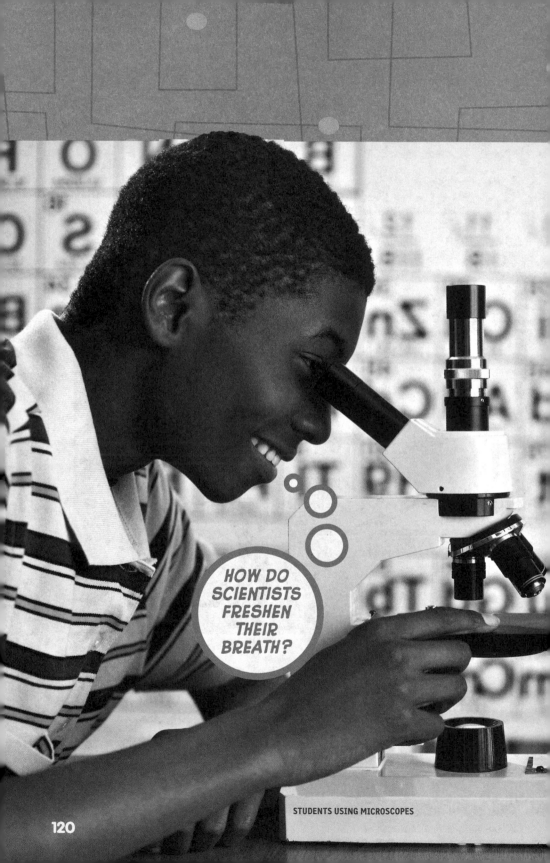

HOW DO
SCIENTISTS
FRESHEN
THEIR
BREATH?

STUDENTS USING MICROSCOPES

# INSPIRED BY NATURE

VELCRO

**1** What inspired Swiss engineer Georges de Mestral to invent Velcro?

**a.** wasp exoskeletons    **c.** loopy moss
**b.** spiky seed pods    **d.** pineapple skins

**2** New high-tech material based on shark's skin has helped athletes in the Olympic sport of _____.

**a.** wrestling          **c.** running
**b.** ice dancing      **d.** swimming

**3** Which desert critter inspired the design of surfaces that draw in water from desert fog?

**a.** ostrich               **c.** African ground squirrel
**b.** Namibian desert beetle    **d.** western rattlesnake

**4** By copying the small bumps on humpback whale fins, engineers made which technology more efficient?

**a.** wind turbine blades
**b.** cell phone battery shells
**c.** wireless Internet receivers
**d.** car engines

HUMPBACK WHALE

**5** True or false?

The number of petals in flowers, leaves on a branch, and seeds in a fruit always follows the same mathematical patterns, such as 1, 2, 4, 8, 16, and so on.

ROSE

**6** The feet of a _____ inspired a device that sticks heavy things to walls.

**a.** gecko       **c.** mountain goat
**b.** turtle       **d.** kangaroo mouse

**7** What does the Eastgate Center in Zimbabwe have in place of air-conditioning?

a. a waterfall in the lobby that makes chilly mist
b. melting ice sculptures
c. gigantic ceiling fans
d. architecture inspired by self-cooling termite mounds

CONE SNAIL

**8** Cone snail venom inspired researchers to create a _____.

a. chemical weapon
b. colorful dye
c. powerful painkiller
d. shark-proof spray

BULLET TRAIN

**9** The pointed nose of Japan's Shinkansen bullet train, designed to reduce noise, is copied from which speedy animal?

a. cheetah
b. dolphin
c. sailfish
d. kingfisher

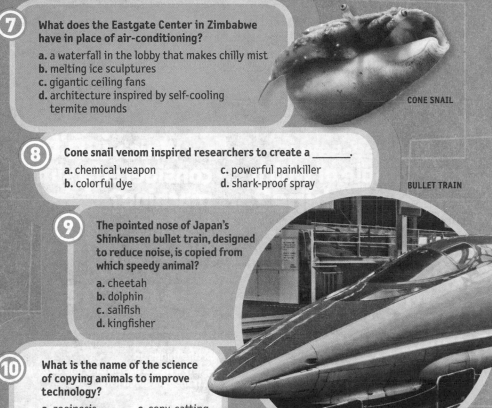

**10** What is the name of the science of copying animals to improve technology?

a. zooinosis
b. bioscanning
c. copy-catting
d. biomimicry

**11** Studying the way butterfly wings produce colors, a company developed new _____.

a. color-changing helmets
b. tie-dyed sunglasses
c. color screens for electronic devices
d. colored silly string

PEACOCK BUTTERFLY

**12** The UltraCane helps blind people navigate with echolocation, just like which animal?

a. spider
b. bat
c. frog
d. lion

# SIMPLE MACHINES

**1** The see-saw is an example of which type of **machine?**

a. lever
b. pulley
c. crank
d. motor

**2** Which **isn't** considered a simple machine?

a. wheel and axle
b. inclined plane
c. screw
d. electrical circuit

**3** Which **tool** uses a wedge to force things apart?

a. ax
b. drill
c. staple gun
d. ladder

**4** A **ratchet** _____.

a. makes a giant explosion
b. lifts things up
c. lets a wheel turn in only one direction
d. transmits electricity

**5** True or false? Adding more pulleys to a rope system makes it easier to lift **heavy** loads.

**6** Which **tool** is made of an inclined plane wrapped into a spiral shape?

a. screw
b. hammer
c. tape measure
d. saw

**7** Which simple machine can you find on a **bicycle?**

a. lever      c. wheel and axle
b. pulley      d. all of the above

**8** Which household object **doesn't** use any simple machine?

a. lightbulb      c. pillow
b. scissors      d. door knob

**9** True or false? A wheelbarrow is an **example** of a compound machine.

**10** Archimedes once said: "Give me a place to stand and with a _____ I will **move** the whole world."

a. lever      c. wheel
b. ramp      d. rocket ship

**11** A **lever** rotates around a _____ .

a. ball bearing      c. fulcrum
b. gear      d. spatula

**12** True or false? A car has exactly four wheel-and-axle **systems.**

**13** Which simple machine would help you **raise** the sails on a boat?

a. wedge      c. screw
b. lever      d. pulley

**14** Your front teeth are an **example** of which machine?

a. pulley
b. wedge
c. gears
d. wheel

# SUPER STAR

**1** What is the name for the outer atmosphere of the sun?

**a.** crust    **c.** corona
**b.** flameball    **d.** black hole

**2** How many sunspots are there on the surface of the sun?

**a.** exactly 371
**b.** between 1,000 and 5,000
**c.** between 500,000 and 1 million
**d.** anywhere from none to over 100

**3** True or false?
The sun stays stationary at the center of the solar system.

**4** The most common element inside the sun is _____ .

**a.** hydrogen    **c.** phosphorous
**b.** iron    **d.** calcium

**5** What problem can a strong storm on the sun cause on Earth?

**a.** volcanic eruptions
**b.** loss of electricity
**c.** zombie uprisings
**d.** all of the above

**6** Most of the matter inside the sun is in which state?

**a.** solid    **c.** gas
**b.** liquid    **d.** plasma

THE SUN

**7** Solar flares are _____.

a. explosions on the sun
b. purple fireworks
c. robots that explore the sun
d. x-ray vision sunglasses

**8** True or false?
A dedicated spacecraft watches the sun at all times.

**9** What do solar panels do?

a. protect animals from sunburn
b. make magnets more powerful
c. convert sunlight into electricity
d. play hip-hop music

**10** Which planet orbits closest to the sun?

a. Venus
b. Earth
c. Mercury
d. Jupiter

**11** Scientists who study the inside of the sun are called _____.

a. geophysicists
b. helioseismologists
c. chemists
d. stargazers

**12** How long does it take light to get from the sun to Earth's surface?

a. under 1 second
b. about 8 minutes
c. exactly 3 days
d. more than 2 years

**13** True or false?
The sun makes up 99 percent of the total mass of our solar system.

# MAP MANIA!
# ANIMAL RESCUE!

## 1 OIL-COVERED BROWN PELICANS

**Volunteers cleaned brown pelicans after the Deepwater Horizon oil spill—the worst in U.S. history. How does oil harm the birds?**

a. It poisons them.
b. It makes them drown.
c. It makes them get too cold.
d. all of the above

NORTH AMERICA

C

F

ATLANTIC OCEAN

PACIFIC OCEAN

E

SOUTH AMERICA

## 2 ELEPHANT POACHING

**National parks work to protect elephants from illegal poaching. What do the poachers want?**

a. elephants' ivory tusks to sell
b. elephants' hides to sell
c. elephants to use as circus animals
d. baby elephants to keep as pets

## 3 SEA TURTLES WASHED ASHORE

**Volunteers search and care for stunned sea turtles that drift ashore each year in early autumn. What causes this problem?**

a. jellyfish stings
b. sailboat accidents
c. sudden cold weather
d. shark attacks

## SHARK FIN SOUP

**4**

A campaign to protect sharks started in 2006 by getting people to not eat shark fin soup. When is the soup traditionally served?

**a.** breakfast  **c.** weddings
**b.** Thanksgiving  **d.** birthday parties

ARCTIC OCEAN

EUROPE

ASIA

AFRICA

PACIFIC
OCEAN

**D**

**A**

INDIAN
OCEAN

**B**

ANTARCTICA

## ILLEGAL PARROT TRADE

**5**

Laws protect wild parrots from illegal capture, but people continue to catch and sell the birds. Where do most of them end up?

**a.** in zoos
**b.** as pets
**c.** as feathered hats
**d.** on farms

## KANGAROOS STRANDED BY FLOODS

**6**

How did people help save kangaroos stranded by heavy flooding in 2011?

**a.** diverted the water
**b.** built bridges
**c.** rescued them in boats
**d.** airlifted them in helicopters

**7–12**

MATCH EACH ANIMAL RESCUE STORY WITH THE LOCATION ON THE MAP WHERE IT HAPPENED.

# EUREKA!

1. THOMAS EDISON WROTE THE FAMOUS EQUATION $E=MC^2$.

2. PAPER WAS INVENTED IN ANCIENT EGYPT.

3. THE WORD "BRAINSTORM" COMES FROM A BEATLES SONG.

4. THE FIRST iPOD CAME OUT IN 2001.

5. GOOSE ISLAND IS HOME TO NEARLY 1,000 GIANT STONE HEADS.

6. EUREKA WAS THE NAME OF THE FIRST RUSSIAN SPACE ROCKET.

7. TO DRIVE A SEGWAY, YOU SIMPLY LEAN FORWARD OR BACKWARD.

8. CHARLES DARWIN BRED PIGEONS TO HELP PROVE HIS THEORY OF EVOLUTION.

9. "EUREKA!" MEANS "YOU'RE CRAZY!" IN GREEK.

10. THE FIRST CALL FROM A CELL PHONE WAS MADE IN 2005.

11. DAGUERREOTYPES ARE EARLY PHOTOGRAPHS.

12. THE NUMBER ZERO WAS INTRODUCED IN THE 16TH CENTURY.

13. INVENTORS THOMAS EDISON AND NIKOLA TESLA WERE RIVALS.

14. AN ACCIDENTAL DISCOVERY AT A MILITARY RESEARCH LAB LED TO THE INVENTION OF THE MICROWAVE OVEN.

15. GALILEO DISCOVERED THE MOONS OF JUPITER.

**16** NEUROSCIENTIST OTTO LOEWI WON A NOBEL PRIZE IN MEDICINE FOR HIS WORK BASED ON AN IDEA THAT CAME TO HIM IN A DREAM.

**17** WHEN MATCHES WERE FIRST INVENTED THEY WERE POISONOUS.

**18** MARIE CURIE IS FAMOUS FOR HER RESEARCH ON STEAM ENGINES.

**19** A POWERFUL ANTIBIOTIC ORIGINALLY CAME FROM A ROTTEN MELON.

**20** BENJAMIN FRANKLIN DISCOVERED ELECTRICITY.

**21** PLAY-DOH WAS ORIGINALLY DEVELOPED TO CLEAN WALLPAPER.

**22** YOU'D HAVE TO TIME-TRAVEL TO EARLY CHINA TO SEE THE WORLD'S FIRST FIREWORKS.

**23** NICOLAUS COPERNICUS IS FAMOUS FOR HIS CONTRIBUTIONS TO COMPUTER SCIENCE.

**24** ASTRONAUTS ONCE USED DUCT TAPE TO REPAIR A MOONBUGGY.

**25** A ROOMBA IS A ROBOT THAT COOKS MEALS.

**26** THE FORD MODEL T WAS THE FIRST MASS-PRODUCED CAR MADE WITH A MOVING ASSEMBLY LINE.

**27** THE FIRST FLASHLIGHTS SHONE FOR ONLY A FEW SECONDS AT A TIME.

**28** THE COMPANY TWITTER WAS ORIGINALLY NAMED ZOOSTER.

**29** A SHEEP WAS THE FIRST ADULT MAMMAL TO BE CLONED.

**30** THE AMAZON KINDLE WAS THE FIRST E-BOOK READER.

CHECK YOUR ANSWERS ON PAGES 166–168.

# CRETACEOUS GIANTS

**1** During which time period did dinosaurs first evolve?

a. Permian
b. Triassic
c. Jurassic
d. Cretaceous

**2** What dinosaur record did *Coahuilaceratops* set when it was discovered?

a. oldest skeleton
b. biggest feet
c. most teeth
d. longest horns

**3** Where did *Coahuilaceratops* live?

a. Mexico
b. Antarctica
c. China
d. Canada

**4** What did many ankylosaur dinosaurs have at the end of their tails?

a. wings
b. poison barbs
c. a club
d. feathers

**5** True or false?
All prehistoric giant animals laid eggs.

**6** Scientists think velociraptors were intelligent because they _____ .

a. acted smart in *Jurassic Park*
b. left behind stone carvings
c. could run really fast
d. had a large brain for their body size

**7** This feathered meat-eater was an early relative of which other dinosaur?

a. *Tyrannosaurus rex*
b. *Iguanodon*
c. *Stegosaurus*
d. *Triceratops*

**8** True or false?
This dinosaur is a *Brontosaurus*.

**9** How was it possible for sauropods like this one to have such long necks?
a. they ate plants not meat
b. they had double spines for support
c. their neck bones were hollow
d. gravity was weaker back then

**10** What was the most unique feature of the Hadrosaur dinosaurs?
a. spiked tail
b. long neck
c. a second brain in its tail
d. duck-like bill

**11** True or false?
Dinosaurs lived on the continent Antarctica during the Cretaceous period.

**12** *Dreadnoughtus* may be the largest dinosaur ever. What does its name mean in Old English?
a. terrible cow
b. afraid of nuts
c. big foot
d. fearing nothing

**13** One tooth from an *Iguanodon* was about the same size as a
_____.
a. strawberry
b. human hand
c. pineapple
d. chicken

**DINOSAURS OF THE CRETACEOUS PERIOD**

CHECK YOUR ANSWERS ON PAGES 166–168.

# NOSING AROUND

PROBOSCIS MONKEY

**1** Why do proboscis monkeys have such large noses?
a. to smell flowers
b. to scare off lions
c. to attract mates
d. to produce extra boogers

**2** Which animal doesn't have a nose?
a. jellyfish
b. dolphin
c. kangaroo
d. frog

**3** The carrion-eating _____ has no sense of smell.
a. fox
b. hyena
c. vulture
d. warthog

**4** What does "rhinoceros," which comes from the Greek language, translate to?
a. knife face
b. nose horn
c. big honker
d. super sniffer

HONEYBEE

**5** A honeybee uses its _____ to detect odors.
a. antennae
b. feet
c. wings
d. stinger

**6** True or false?

Trained rats use their super sense of smell to sniff out hidden landmines in Africa.

**7** A _____ has a better sense of smell than a dog.

a. rabbit    c. squirrel
b. bear    d. human

**8** Which animal does this stellar nose belong to?

a. crab    c. mole
b. platypus    d. opossum

ASIAN
ELEPHANTS

**9** Which isn't a real animal with a big snout?

a. unicornfish    c. Pinocchio lizard
b. tube-nosed bat    d. blue-nose goat

**10** Snub-nosed monkeys live in _____.

a. Africa
b. Australia
c. North America
d. Asia

**11** True or false?

A dog could smell a single teaspoon of sugar dissolved in a million gallons of water.

**12** What color is a mandrill monkey's nose?

a. bright red and blue
b. dark brown
c. white with pink spots
d. light green

**13** True or false?

The elephant is the only animal with a trunk.

# IT'S ELEMENTAL

**1** Where in the U.S.A. did people rush to find **gold** in the mid-1800s?

a. Florida     c. California
b. Idaho     d. Maine

**2** Superman's home **planet** has the same name as which element on the Periodic Table?

a. krypton     c. zinc
b. argon     d. selenium

**3** Which of these **fruits** contains the most potassium per serving?

a. apple     c. pineapple
b. blueberries     d. banana

**4** What **color** do copper pennies often turn as they age?

a. green
b. blue
c. yellow
d. They never change color.

**5** Which **element** makes your birthday balloons float in the air?

a. oxygen     c. calcium
b. helium     d. xenon

**6** True or false? All glowing advertising **signs** contain the element neon.

**7** Why **shouldn't** you use a mercury thermometer?

a. Mercury explodes.     c. Mercury is poisonous.
b. It's too expensive.     d. It's not very accurate.

**8** The **name** Silicon Valley comes from

_____.

a. the words "silly" and "conference"
b. the element in computer chips
c. the silver coins that were made there
d. trillionaire Sylvester Silicon

**9** What is the name for a **person** who did chemistry experiments during the Middle Ages?

a. sorcerer          c. kamikaze
b. duchess           d. alchemist

**10** Which **scientist** developed the Periodic Table of Elements?

a. Charles Darwin      c. Isaac Newton
b. Louis Pasteur       d. Dmitri Mendeleev

**11** The element _____ gives **atomic** bombs their explosive power.

a. hydrogen          c. phosphorous
b. plutonium         d. boron

**12** True or false? All of the elements on the Periodic Table can be found in **nature.**

**13** What element do diamonds, frogs, and **coal** have in common?

a. carbon
b. antimony
c. uranium
d. helium

**14** True or false? **Beethoven** suffered from lead poisoning.

# GAME SHOW

# ULTIMATE SCIENCE CHALLENGE

**1** Which scientist was the first to see and identify distant galaxies?
a. Leonardo Da Vinci
b. Edwin Hubble
c. Jane Goodall
d. Thomas Edison

**2** ## TRUE OR FALSE?
The bearcat smells like buttered popcorn.

**3** ## TRUE OR FALSE?
*Tyrannosaurus rex* walked upright, with its tail dragging on the ground.

**4** What could cause this fish to lose its sense of smell?
a. strong hurricane winds
b. eating hot peppers
c. polluting chemicals in the water
d. nothing; fish don't have noses

**5** Another name for the element mercury is _____.
a. quicksilver
b. liquid iron
c. hot ice
d. magic show

**6** Which female scientist helped find the chemical structure of DNA?
a. Rachel Carson
b. Rosalind Franklin
c. Mary Anning
d. Marie Curie

**7** This doorknob is an example of which simple machine?
a. lever
b. wheel and axle
c. pulley
d. all of the above

**8** Too much exposure to the ultraviolet radiation in sunlight can cause which disease?

a. blindness
b. measles
c. the flu
d. cancer

**9** **TRUE OR FALSE?**

Inventor Doug Engelbart's pet mouse inspired his invention of the computer mouse.

**10** Which simple machine makes a playground slide so much fun?

a. lever
b. gears
c. inclined plane
d. wedge

**11** Dogs are helping protect endangered tigers by _____.

a. fighting off snakes that attack tigers
b. raising tiger cubs
c. catching prey to feed to tigers
d. sniffing out tiger poop to locate wild tigers

**12** In what kind of habitat did the giant sail-back dinosaur *Spinosaurus* live?

a. water and land
b. desert
c. mountain cliffs
d. treetops

**13** During a total solar eclipse, _____.

a. Earth turns away from the sun
b. the moon blocks the sun
c. Venus and Mars line up with the sun
d. all of the above

**14** Until Jonas Salk invented a vaccine for it, which disease disabled many children?

a. chicken pox     c. lyme disease
b. malaria          d. polio

**15** What is this dinosaur called?

a. *Iguanodon*
b. *Diplodocus*
c. *Parasaurolophus*
d. *Spoonheadupus*

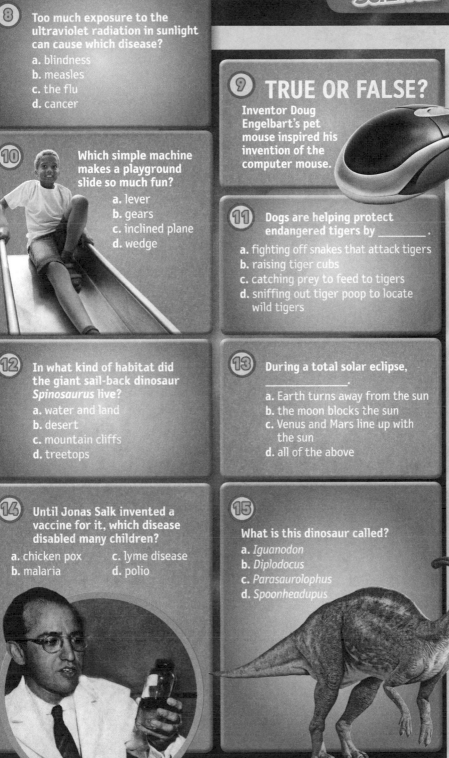

CHECK YOUR ANSWERS ON PAGES 166–168.

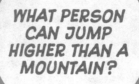

WHAT PERSON
CAN JUMP
HIGHER THAN A
MOUNTAIN?

BASE JUMPING OFF A CLIFF

# To the RESCUE!

SMOKEJUMPER

**1** **True or false?** The international distress signal SOS doesn't stand for anything.

**2** **What type of rescue worker is a smokejumper?**
a. earthquake paramedic
b. fireworks nurse
c. forest firefighter
d. volcano skydiver

**3** Providing enough lifeboats to accommodate all passengers aboard a ship became a requirement after the sinking of the _____ .
a. R.M.S. *Lusitania*
b. *Mary Celeste*
c. R.M.S. *Titanic*
d. *Whydah Gally*

**4** **True or false?** In North America, a police dog is often called a K-9.

**5** **Who would most likely come to the rescue of a passenger who had fallen off a ship in U.S. waters?**
a. Navy
b. Army
c. Coast Guard
d. hall monitors

POLICE DOG

**6** **Which of the following is *not* a step in CPR?**
a. Check the victim for signs of breathing.
b. Pump the victim's chest.
c. Blow into the victim's mouth.
d. Look into the victim's ears.

**7** **Robots designed to mimic which animal are used to rescue people trapped under rubble?**
a. sloth
b. panda
c. snake
d. frog

**8** The nickname Mounties is used to describe which country's police force?
a. Canada
b. Iceland
c. Uruguay
d. Morocco

**9** Think fast! If you're caught in an avalanche, which activity can help you stay close to the surface of the snow?
a. a swimming motion
b. jumping jacks
c. somersaults
d. push-ups

DANGER AVALANCHE

**10** In the event of an emergency, what part of an airplane seat can be used as a flotation device?
a. food tray
b. seat cushion
c. headrest
d. seat pocket

MOUNTIE

**11** If you're lost without a compass at night, you can get a sense of direction by looking for which star?
a. sun
b. Sirius
c. Polaris
d. Vega

**12** True or false? If you're stranded on a desert island, you should never drink salt water.

DALMATIAN

**13** Which car company introduced the three-point seat belt that's still used today?
a. Volvo
b. Ford
c. Rolls-Royce
d. Mazda

**14** True or false? Dalmatians are used by fire departments because they can detect fire.

CHECK YOUR ANSWERS ON PAGES 168–170.

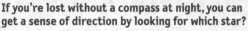

# TRUE or FALSE?

# Parks of the World

**1** LECHUGUILLA CAVE IN CARLSBAD CAVERNS NATIONAL PARK, NEW MEXICO, U.S.A., IS DEEPER THAN THE EMPIRE STATE BUILDING IS TALL.

**2** THE WORLD'S TALLEST TREE CAN BE FOUND IN INDIA'S JIM CORBETT NATIONAL PARK.

**3** GUATEMALA'S TIKAL NATIONAL PARK WAS ONCE HOME TO THE ANCIENT MAYA.

**4** THERE IS A ROCK FORMATION IN BRYCE CANYON NATIONAL PARK, UTAH, U.S.A., THAT IS SHAPED LIKE AN INDIAN PRINCESS.

**5** GOLDEN GATE PARK IN CALIFORNIA, U.S.A., WAS CREATED AS AN ESCAPE FOR PEOPLE WHO NEEDED A BREAK FROM CITY LIFE IN SAN FRANCISCO.

**6** PRESIDENT WILLIAM J. CLINTON WAS THE FIRST TO ESTABLISH A NATIONAL PARK IN THE UNITED STATES.

**7** OLD FAITHFUL, A GEYSER IN YELLOWSTONE NATIONAL PARK, U.S.A., GOT ITS NAME BECAUSE IT SPOUTS WATER AT PREDICTABLE INTERVALS.

**8** OLYMPIC NATIONAL PARK IN WASHINGTON, U.S.A., IS NAMED FOR THE OLYMPICS, WHICH WERE ONCE HOSTED IN THE STATE.

**9** THE WORLD'S HOTTEST TEMPERATURE WAS RECORDED IN DEATH VALLEY NATIONAL PARK, CALIFORNIA, U.S.A.

**10** KLUANE NATIONAL PARK AND RESERVE OF CANADA IS HOME TO THE COUNTRY'S TALLEST MOUNTAIN.

**11** JAPAN'S LARGEST ACTIVE VOLCANO IS LOCATED IN A NATIONAL PARK.

**12** ANGEL FALLS, IN VENEZUELA'S CANAIMA NATIONAL PARK, IS TALLER THAN THE WORLD'S TALLEST BUILDING.

**13** THE BLUE-FOOTED BOOBY IS A BIRD THAT CAN BE FOUND ONLY IN EAST ANGLIA, ENGLAND.

**14** DENALI NATIONAL PARK AND PRESERVE IN ALASKA, U.S.A., IS LARGER THAN THE STATE OF NEW HAMPSHIRE.

**15** EACH YEAR, MORE THAN ONE MILLION WILDEBEEST ARRIVE IN TANZANIA'S SERENGETI NATIONAL PARK.

**16** THE GRAND CANYON, IN ARIZONA, U.S.A., WAS CARVED OUT BY A RIVER.

**17** DARK SKY PARKS ARE PLACES WHERE YOU CAN SEE EXCEPTIONALLY STARRY SKIES.

**18** YOU CAN SEE PENGUINS AT THE ISLA MAGDALENA NATIONAL PARK IN CHILE.

**19** WATERTON-GLACIER INTERNATIONAL PEACE PARK WAS THE FIRST PARK TO SPAN THE BORDER OF TWO COUNTRIES.

**20** THE STATUE OF LIBERTY IS LOCATED IN A U.S. NATIONAL PARK.

**21** KAKADU NATIONAL PARK IN AUSTRALIA IS HOME TO CHEROKEE INDIANS.

**22** THE WORLD'S LARGEST NATIONAL PARK IS BIGGER THAN ITALY.

**23** MAMMOTH CAVE NATIONAL PARK IN KENTUCKY, U.S.A., WAS NAMED FOR A WOOLLY MAMMOTH FOSSIL THAT WAS DISCOVERED THERE.

**24** MOUNT EVEREST IS PART OF A NATIONAL PARK.

**25** DINOSAURS ONCE ROAMED ACROSS AN AREA IN ARGENTINA THAT IS NOW A NATIONAL PARK.

**26** THERE IS A NATIONAL PARK IN EVERY U.S. STATE.

**27** CANADA'S BANFF NATIONAL PARK IS HOME TO A SPECIES OF FLYING CARIBOU.

**28** PANDORA, THE FICTIONAL WORLD IN THE MOVIE *AVATAR*, WAS INSPIRED BY A NATIONAL PARK IN CHINA.

**29** THE FJORDS OF FIORDLAND NATIONAL PARK IN NEW ZEALAND ARE A TYPE OF GLACIER.

**30** ONLY MALE TSAVO LIONS OF KENYA'S TSAVO NATIONAL PARKS HAVE MANES.

CHECK YOUR ANSWERS ON PAGES 168–170.

# SPY SCHOOL

**1** What type of bird was used to transport **secret** messages until the 1950s?

a. bluebird
b. pigeon
c. hummingbird
d. flamingo

**2** The **word** "espionage" comes from the French word *espionner*, which means _____.

a. to disguise
b. to keep a secret
c. to spy
d. to trick

**3** What does the word "bug" mean to a spy?

a. an annoying person
b. a listening device
c. a double agent
d. a secret mission

**4** What is the name for a secret identity used by spies?

a. legend
b. cover
c. agent
d. code

**5** Which of these spies from **movies** did NOT get their start as book characters?

a. Harriet the Spy
b. James Bond
c. Alex Rider
d. Agent Cody Banks

**6** Which language, used by the American forces in World War II to communicate secret messages, was indecipherable by its **enemies?**

a. Italian
b. German
c. Navajo
d. Pig Latin

**7** What part of a submarine is used to **spy** on ships that are on the water's surface?

a. periscope
b. telescope
c. binoculars
d. magnifying glass

**8** What would a spy do with a cipher?

a. send secret messages
b. follow suspicious cars
c. poison enemies
d. open locked doors

**9** The KGB was which country's intelligence agency until 1991?

a. Soviet Union
b. United States
c. Switzerland
d. Japan

**10** The **Culper Ring** provided which American leader with information during the Revolutionary War?

a. John Adams
b. James Madison
c. George Washington
d. Abraham Lincoln

**11** A spy who gets "deep" into an organization in order to share its **secrets** with a rival organization is known as a _____.

a. giraffe
b. canary
c. mole
d. ladybug

**12** True or false?

Some **spy** satellites can view newspaper headlines from space.

**13** The secret location where one **spy** leaves a message for another spy is called a _____.

a. dead drop
b. sleeper
c. target
d. letter box

# TOMB RAIDER

**2** What ancient structure was built for Khufu, an Egyptian pharaoh?
a. Temple of Luxor
b. Cleopatra's Needle
c. Great Pyramid at Giza
d. Abu Simbel in Nubia

**1** You're most likely to find jewelry in the shape of which insect in an ancient Egyptian tomb?
a. butterfly
b. scarab beetle
c. ladybug
d. praying mantis

**3** All of the following rooms can be found in the Great Pyramid of Giza except the _____.
a. King's Chamber
b. Grand Gallery
c. Queen's Chamber
d. Dining Hall

**4** This coffin is called a ___.
a. sarcophagus
b. cartouche
c. sphinx
d. ziggurat

**5** What item was not discovered in King Tutankhamun's tomb?
a. underwear     c. chariots
b. books          d. jewels

**6** True or false? Ancient Egyptian rulers were buried with items that they wanted to take with them to the afterlife.

**7** What ancient form of writing was often found inside Egyptian tombs?
a. Cyrillic       c. cuneiform
b. hieroglyphics  d. Sanskrit

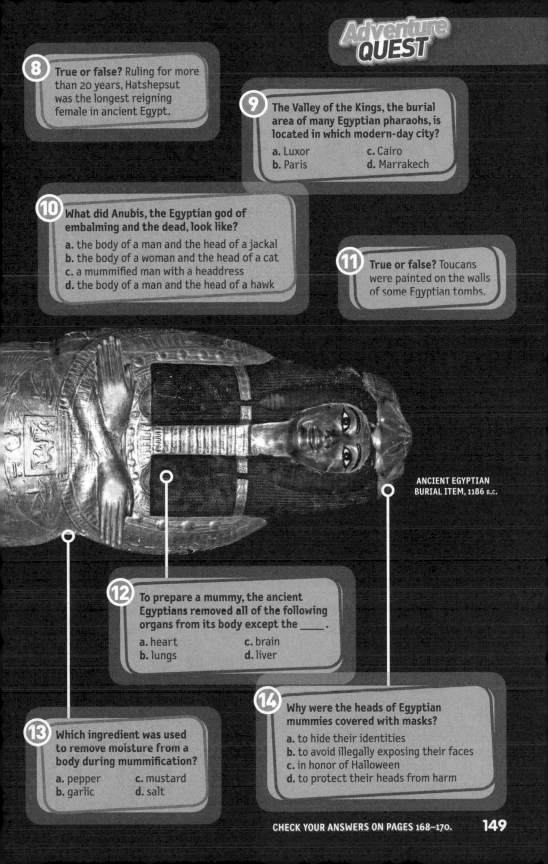

**8** **True or false?** Ruling for more than 20 years, Hatshepsut was the longest reigning female in ancient Egypt.

**9** The Valley of the Kings, the burial area of many Egyptian pharaohs, is located in which modern-day city?
a. Luxor      c. Cairo
b. Paris      d. Marrakech

**10** What did Anubis, the Egyptian god of embalming and the dead, look like?
a. the body of a man and the head of a jackal
b. the body of a woman and the head of a cat
c. a mummified man with a headdress
d. the body of a man and the head of a hawk

**11** **True or false?** Toucans were painted on the walls of some Egyptian tombs.

ANCIENT EGYPTIAN
BURIAL ITEM, 1186 B.C.

**12** To prepare a mummy, the ancient Egyptians removed all of the following organs from its body except the ____.
a. heart      c. brain
b. lungs      d. liver

**13** Which ingredient was used to remove moisture from a body during mummification?
a. pepper      c. mustard
b. garlic      d. salt

**14** Why were the heads of Egyptian mummies covered with masks?
a. to hide their identities
b. to avoid illegally exposing their faces
c. in honor of Halloween
d. to protect their heads from harm

CHECK YOUR ANSWERS ON PAGES 168–170.

# THE ADVENTURES OF MARCO POLO

**1** **Marco Polo** was a European explorer in the 1200s famous for his travels to China. He was originally from _____.

a. Spain
b. Italy
c. Germany
d. Ireland

**2** The route he took to reach present-day **China** was known as the _____.

a. Silk Road
b. Atlantic Road
c. Abbey Road
d. Yellow Brick Road

**3** Which desert did Marco Polo have to cross to get to China?

a. Gobi
b. Sahara
c. Sonoran
d. Atacama

**4** Which animal did Marco Polo mistake for a **unicorn**?

a. Siberian tiger
b. Asian elephant
c. rhinoceros
d. reindeer

**5** The Polos were a **family** of _____.

a. doctors
b. merchants
c. politicans
d. chefs

**6** True or false? Marco Polo was the first European traveler to **reach** China.

**7** To what invention did the Chinese introduce Marco Polo?

a. gunpowder
b. cheese
c. the printing press
d. glue

CHECK YOUR ANSWERS ON PAGES 168–170.

**8** The **emperor** of China had Marco Polo do all of the following jobs except _____.

a. tax inspector
b. messenger
c. governor
d. butler

**9** What famous fierce ruler was Kublai Khan's grandfather?

a. Attila the Hun
b. Alexander the Great
c. Genghis Khan
d. Ramesses II

**10** **According** to Marco Polo, what did the Mongol people of Asia use instead of paper money?

a. chocolate
b. silver
c. berries
d. salt

**11** Which **famous** explorer was inspired by Marco Polo's travels?

a. James Cook
b. Christopher Columbus
c. Henry Hudson
d. Neil Armstrong

**12** About how many years did Marco Polo spend in **China**?

a. 1 year
b. 8 years
c. 12 years
d. 17 years

**13** True or false? No other explorer has ever traveled a greater **distance** than Marco Polo.

MARCO POLO WITH A CARAVAN; ILLUSTRATION FROM THE *CATALAN ATLAS*, AROUND 1375

# The EVERGLADES

**1** What is the name of this popular mode of transportation for exploring the Everglades?

**a.** airboat
**b.** watertruck
**c.** surfboard
**d.** ferry

EVERGLADES
TRANSPORTATION

**2** What U.S. president dedicated Everglades National Park in 1947?

**a.** Harry S. Truman
**c.** John F. Kennedy
**b.** Abraham Lincoln
**d.** Ronald Reagan

**3** In which U.S. state are the Everglades located?

**a.** California
**b.** Mississippi
**c.** Florida
**d.** Alaska

**4** Which invasive species has been attacking the native wildlife of the Everglades?

**a.** leatherback sea turtle
**b.** key deer
**c.** Burmese python
**d.** kangaroo

**5** Who were some of the first people to call the Everglades home?

**a.** Calusa Indians
**c.** Vikings
**b.** Spanish explorers
**d.** English colonists

**6** Mangrove trees help protect the Everglades from _____ .

**a.** animal invaders
**b.** the sun's ultraviolet (UV) rays
**c.** hurricane storm surges
**d.** traffic

**7** True or false? The Everglades is the only place on Earth where the American alligator and the American crocodile coexist.

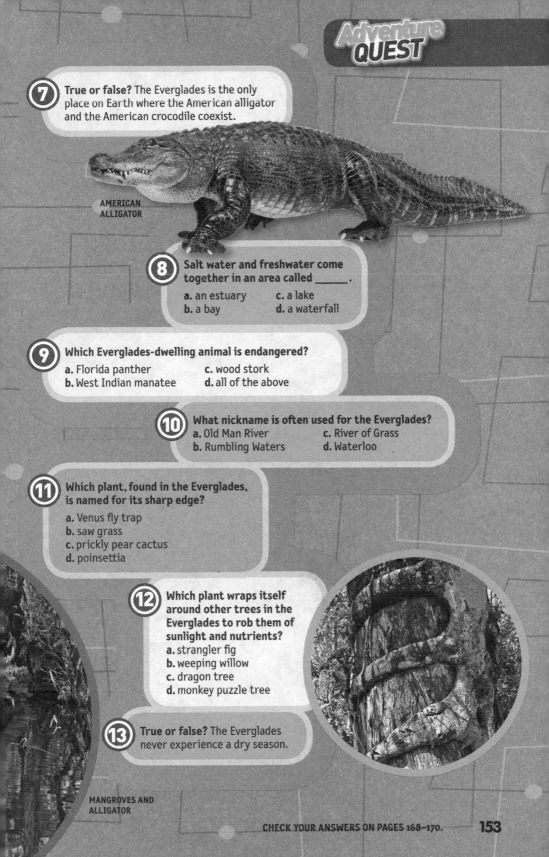

AMERICAN ALLIGATOR

**8** Salt water and freshwater come together in an area called _____.
- **a.** an estuary
- **b.** a bay
- **c.** a lake
- **d.** a waterfall

**9** Which Everglades-dwelling animal is endangered?
- **a.** Florida panther
- **b.** West Indian manatee
- **c.** wood stork
- **d.** all of the above

**10** What nickname is often used for the Everglades?
- **a.** Old Man River
- **b.** Rumbling Waters
- **c.** River of Grass
- **d.** Waterloo

**11** Which plant, found in the Everglades, is named for its sharp edge?
- **a.** Venus fly trap
- **b.** saw grass
- **c.** prickly pear cactus
- **d.** poinsettia

**12** Which plant wraps itself around other trees in the Everglades to rob them of sunlight and nutrients?
- **a.** strangler fig
- **b.** weeping willow
- **c.** dragon tree
- **d.** monkey puzzle tree

**13** True or false? The Everglades never experience a dry season.

MANGROVES AND ALLIGATOR

CHECK YOUR ANSWERS ON PAGES 168–170.

# MAP MANIA!
# CELEBRATE OUTDOORS

**M**any countries have fantastic festivals that take place outdoors. How well do you know them? Answer these questions to find out.

## 1 UNITED STATES

Each spring, the National Cherry Blossom Festival celebrates the blooming of cherry trees that were originally a gift from _____.

**a.** Germany    **c.** Brazil
**b.** Ireland    **d.** Japan

NORTH AMERICA

ATLANTIC OCEAN

PACIFIC OCEAN

SOUTH AMERICA

C
E
A
D
B

## 2 PORTUGAL

At the International Sand Sculpture Festival, artists are given a theme to follow. Based on this photo, what was the theme for the year?

**a.** famous sportspeople
**b.** animals
**c.** music
**d.** mythical creatures

## 3 ENGLAND

Participants in the Bristol Balloon Fiesta fly aboard hot-air balloons while standing inside a basket called a _____.

**a.** gondola    **c.** car
**b.** bucket    **d.** elevator

## 4 CHINA

At the Harbin International Ice and Snow Sculpture Festival, the art covers an area the size of _____ .
a. Disneyland, U.S.A.       c. Times Square, U.S.A.
b. Pyramid of Giza, Egypt   d. Lake Victoria, Africa

ARCTIC OCEAN

EUROPE

ASIA

F

AFRICA

G

PACIFIC OCEAN

INDIAN OCEAN

ANTARCTICA

## Adventure QUEST

## 5 SPAIN

La Tomatina, the world's biggest tomato fight, cannot begin until someone climbs up a greased pole to retrieve _____ .

a. salad dressing
b. a ham
c. salt and pepper
d. a pizza

## 6 BRAZIL

What is the most common music played during Carnival in Rio de Janeiro?

a. jazz
b. country
c. samba
d. hip-hop

## 7 INDIA

The Hindu festival of Holi is sometimes called the _____ .

a. Festival of Colors
b. Festival of Water
c. Festival of Lights
d. Festival of Fire

## 8-14
MATCH EACH LETTER ON THE HIGHLIGHTED AREAS ON THE MAP WITH A NUMBER OF A COUNTRY MENTIONED IN QUESTIONS 1–7.

CHECK YOUR ANSWERS ON PAGES 168–170.

# GAME SHOW

# ULTIMATE ADVENTURE CHALLENGE

**1** Which animal, nicknamed the sea cow, calls the Everglades home?
a. dolphin       c. beaver
b. manatee       d. blue whale

**2** People who settled in the Everglades were known as _____.
a. Forty-niners
b. Gladesmen
c. Barnstormers
d. Marlins

**3** Early in the morning on the first day of spring, the people of Zenica, Bosnia, gather for what food-themed celebration?
a. Festival of Roast Beef
b. Festival of Scrambled Eggs
c. Festival of Chocolate Mousse
d. Festival of Hot Dogs

**4** The Heimlich maneuver is used to help someone who is _____.
a. drowning
b. choking
c. bleeding
d. falling

**5** Mardi Gras, a famous festival in New Orleans, U.S.A., translates to what phrase in English?
a. Slow Sunday
b. Happy Monday
c. Fat Tuesday
d. Wicked Wednesday

**6** The crash test dummy was invented to test the safety of _____.
a. trains
b. boats
c. automobiles
d. bicycles

**7** Which of the following San Francisco, U.S.A., sites is part of Golden Gate National Park?
a. Alcatraz
b. Fisherman's Wharf
c. Golden Gate Bridge
d. Lombard Street

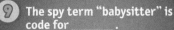

**8** Since spies call a fake passport a "shoe," the person who creates such a passport is a _____.
a. chef
c. tailor
b. cobbler
d. sculptor

**9** The spy term "babysitter" is code for _____.
a. police officer
b. criminal
c. bodyguard
d. mentor

**10** Which former U.S. president has had a national park named after him?
a. Theodore Roosevelt
b. George Washington
c. James Garfield
d. Ronald Reagan

**11 TRUE OR FALSE?**
Marco Polo traveled to the East alone.

**12** What do some experts believe caused the death of King Tut?
a. He was murdered.
b. He was in a chariot accident.
c. He was attacked by a lion.
d. He fell off a pyramid.

**13** If you were drifting in a lifeboat, what may you use to attract the attention of a passing ship?
a. megaphone
b. flare
c. whistle
d. slingshot

**14 ULTIMATE BRAIN BUSTER**
What type of animal at the Brookfield Zoo, in Illinois, U.S.A., once rescued a three-year-old boy who had fallen into its enclosure?

a.
gorilla

b.
bottlenose dolphin

c.
Siberian tiger

d.
brown bear

# ANSWERS

## In the WILD

### Dynamite Dolphins!
#### pages 10–11

1. **False.** River dolphins live only in freshwater.
2. d     3. c     4. b     5. b
6. **True.** Scientists call a dolphin's name its "signature whistle."
7. a
8. **d.** Dolphins get water from the food they eat. In captivity, a dolphin will drink freshwater.
9. **False.** Porpoises are smaller and have a flat face with almost no beak.
10. c     11. d     12. c     13. d
14. **False.** Dolphins are mammals. The mother gives birth to a live calf that drinks its mother's milk.

### Bird Watch,
#### pages 12–13

1. c     2. b     3. b
4. **True.** Female birds tend to prefer brightly colored males.
5. **True.** The male feeds his family through a slit in the side of the nest.
6. d     7. c     8. d     9. a
10. **False.** If an airplane sped up as fast as this bird does, the pilot would pass out!
11. d     12. c

### Creepy Creatures,
#### pages 14–15

1. b     2. b     3. c
4. **False.** Tasmanian devils have no horns; they look like small bears.
5. a     6. b     7. d     8. c
9. **False.** The vampire squid feeds on the waste of fish and other sea creatures.
10. d     11. b     12. b
13. **True.** The lizard's feet and running style keep it from sinking.
14. a

### Animal Acrobats,
#### pages 16–17

1. c     2. a     3. a     4. b
5. d     6. b     7. a
8. **True.** Most kinds of bears can walk on their hind legs.
9. c     10. d
11. **True.** The trunk has more than 100,000 different muscles, and your body has fewer than 800.
12. **False.** All ants have six legs.
13. c

### True or False? It's Classified!
#### pages 18–19

1. **False.** Dolphins and whales are mammals, like you!
2. **False.** Bacteria and fungi are alive, but aren't plants or animals.
3. **True.** Binomial nomenclature uses the genus and the species to refer to a specific creature. A lion is *Panthera leo.*
4. **False.** Carl Linnaeus started developing the classification system in the 1700s.
5. **True.** Arachnida is the animal class that contains spiders and other similar insects.
6. **False.** The echidna—a relative of the platypus—also lays eggs.
7. **True.** Chickens and ostriches are the birds most closely related to *T. rex.*
8. **True.** Humans are most closely related to apes and monkeys.
9. **False.** Most horses and rhinoceroses have one large and two small toes on each foot.
10. **True.** Even bacteria and fungi use DNA to reproduce.
11. **True.** Humans, gorillas, and lemurs are primates, too.
12. **True.** There are about 20,000 different species of ray-finned fishes.
13. **True.** The phylum Chordata contains all animals with a notochord, or flexible spine.
14. **False.** "Amphibian" is Greek for "having two modes of life."
15. **True.** Crocodiles are more closely related to birds than to snakes or lizards.
16. **True.** The Pacific leaping blenny hops around on rocks at the ocean shoreline.
17. **False.** The pygmy mouse lemur grows to about 2.5 inches (6.4 cm) long.
18. **False.** The opossum is native to North America. It has a pouch, just like a kangaroo.
19. **False.** Most starfish have five arms— and some have even more!
20. **True.** All arthropods have segmented bodies.
21. **True.** All mammals also have hair.
22. **True.** Penguins and emus are among birds that have wings but can't fly.
23. **False.** Bats and rodents are classified into separate orders of mammals.
24. **True.** A recent study of their genes revealed this fact.
25. **False.** Armadillos are mammals.
26. **True.** However, some species of lungfish do not use their gills as adults.
27. **False.** Carnivores are meat-eaters. Animals that eat fish are called piscivores.
28. **False.** Moths and butterflies have compound eyes.
29. **True.** Many insectivores also eat roots, plants, fish, or frogs.
30. **True.** Aardvarks live in the wild in southern Africa, where Afrikaans is a common language.

### Chill Out,
#### pages 20–21

1. a
2. **True.** Walruses use their tusks to help them walk on land.
3. d     4. b     5. a     6. c

7. **b**     8. **b**
9. **False.** Many butterfly species live in Alaska.
10. **d**    11. **a**     12. **c**     13. **d**

## Doggone It!
### pages 22–23
1. **d**     2. **d**
3. **False.** Cool, moist air actually makes scents easier to detect.
4. **b**     5. **c**     6. **b**
7. **True.** Dogs have an incredible sense of smell, but can't taste as well as you can.
8. **c**     9. **a**     10. **d**
11. **a**    12. **c**

13. **False.** The Basenji does not bark—it makes a yodeling sound instead.

## Game Show: Ultimate Animal Challenge,
### pages 24–25
1. **d**     2. **a**
3. **True.** Columbus called manatees mermaids, but said that they weren't as beautiful as he expected.
4. **b**     5. **b**     6. **d**
7. **a**     8. **c**     9. **b**
10. **b**    11. **d**    12. **a**

13. **True.** The elephant produces a lot more pee, but it comes out much faster.
14. **c**    15. **c**

# SCORING

## 0–41
### PUPPY LOVE
You adore kittens, puppies, and baby bunnies, but spiders and snakes creep you out. All animals are amazing when you learn more about them. Get to know some insects and crustaceans, and you may make a new friend!

## 42–83
### MIDDLE OF THE PACK
You let others take the lead, but secretly you're smart and cunning, and you look out for your friends—especially the furry kind. Use your smarts to become a veterinarian or animal rescue worker.

## 84–124
### TOP DOG!
You must have the nose of a bloodhound, the ears of a jackrabbit, and the eyes of an eagle to know so much about animals. You win best in show. Keep it up, and you could someday be president of an animal empire.

# Wild WORLD

## Wild World of Sports,
### pages 28–29
1. **b**     2. **d**
3. **False.** She is an American NASCAR race driver.
4. **b**     5. **c**     6. **d**     7. **d**
8. **b**     9. **c**     10. **b**    11. **a**
12. **False.** It is also called Ping-Pong.
13. **True.** *Kabaddi* is the national sport of Bangladesh.

## Alpine Journey,
### pages 30–31
1. **d**     2. **c**     3. **b**
4. **d.** The tunnel will be 35 miles (56.3 km) long when completed.
5. **c**     6. **d**
7. **False.** It is a type of wildflower found here.
8. **True.** All of these trails are located in France.
9. **c**     10. **d**    11. **b**
12. **b**    13. **c**

## True or False? Country Challenge,
### pages 32–33
1. **True.** However, the country has more than 100,000 lakes.
2. **False.** There are 48 countries completely surrounded by land.
3. **False.** It was invented in Denmark.
4. **True.** It is named after the brazilwood tree.
5. **False.** They all came from Italy.
6. **False.** With hundreds of courses, Thailand claims this name.
7. **True.** Belgian comic makers have created Tintin, Asterix, and the Smurfs.
8. **True.** Mount Everest and Annapurna are two of them.
9. **False.** It's France's nickname because of the country's shape.

10. **True.** It is especially known for its tulips.
11. **False.** Madagascar's nickname is the Great Red Island due to its soils.
12. **False.** Morocco is larger than California.
13. **True.** The city of Ushuaia claims this title.
14. **False.** At nearly 4 miles (6.4 km) long, Nanjing Road in China is a shopper's delight.
15. **False.** Iceland elected the world's first female head of state, Vigdís Finnbogadóttir, in 1980.
16. **True.** Aotearoa is the name for New Zealand in the Maori language.
17. **False.** Australia can claim that dubious honor.

18. **True.** Bob Marley was a famous reggae musician from Jamaica.
19. **True.** Comoros produces most of the world's supply of ylang-ylang essence, used in perfumes.
20. **False.** With at least 400 volcanoes (over 130 active), Indonesia has that title.
21. **False.** India's Ramoji Film City is more than 1,666 acres (674 ha) in size.
22. **False.** France has hosted 3 times but the U.S. has hosted 4 Winter Olympics.
23. **True.** Pluto is roughly 6.4 million square miles (16.6 million sq km) in area to Russia's 6.6 million square miles (17 million sq km).
24. **True.** Potatoes are native to the Andes region.
25. **False.** Saolas live in the Annamite Mountains of Laos and Vietnam. They were only discovered in 1992.
26. **True.** These are small savory snacks.
27. **True.** Portuguese is the official language in Brazil (195 million people) and Portugal (10 million people).
28. **True.** All 11 million cattle are given their own ID number to track them.
29. **False.** China has this many bicycles. Bicycles came to China in the 1800s.
30. **False.** With more than 600 castles, Wales can claim this title.

## It's a Sign!
### pages 34–35
1. c  2. a  3. d
4. **False.** But they can be found near Canada's Rideau Canal in Ottawa.
5. b  6. c
7. **True.** *Pare* is seen in Turkey, *arrêt* in French-speaking countries, and *berhenti* in Malaysia.
8. c  9. a  10. c
11. **True.** Oamaru is one New Zealand town where such signs can be found.

## What's for Lunch?
### pages 36–37
1. c
2. **True.** *Ugali* is made from cornmeal, much like the Italian dish polenta.
3. a  4. c  5. c
6. **True.** School kids here normally go home from 12 to 3 p.m. to eat lunch with their families.
7. **True.** More than 5,000 delivery people called *dabbawalas* do this job.
8. b  9. b  10. a  11. d

## Super Celebrations,
### pages 38–39
1. b  2. d  3. c  4. a
5. **True.** They also decorate their tables with round foods—circles symbolize good luck.

6. d  7. b
8. **True.** Japanese women also spoil the men in their lives with other gifts on this holiday.
9. c  10. b
11. **False.** Red is the color of good luck in China.

## Map Mania! Where in the World,
### pages 40-41
1. China  2. United Kingdom
3. Sweden  4. India
5. Turkey  6. Philippines
7. Mexico  8. Nigeria
9. Brazil  10. Australia
11. Russia
12. 1C  13. 2A  14. 3H  15. 4D
16. 5J  17. 6K  18. 7G  19. 8E
20. 9B  21. 10F  22. 11I

## Game Show: Ultimate Geography Challenge,
### pages 42–43
1. b
2. **True.** Hundreds of Papuan and Melanesian tribes call Papua New Guinea home.
3. a  4. c  5. c  6. d
7. d  8. b  9. d
10. **False.** There are more than 21 million registered cats and dogs and 16.5 million children under age 15.
11. b  12. a  13. b
14. **True.** Bakers hide a coin, jewel, or small toy inside this cake.
15. a

# SCORING

### 0–42
## HAPPY HOMEBODY
You may have examined every inch of your backyard, but you could stand to get more familiar with places more than 100 miles (161 km) from home base. Take an out-of-town trip and start exploring the world.

### 43–85
## CULTURE VULTURE
The travel bug has bitten you, but most of your expertise comes from library books. While knowledge is power, you'll do well to get on a plane with your family and practice your French in Paris.

### 86–126
## GLOBE-TROTTING GENIUS
You're ready for a world tour. You can't wait to head to famous locales like Mount Everest and remote regions like the rain forests of Borneo. Exploring cultural sites and gorgeous locations is your top reward.

# Pop CULTURE

## '90s Novelties, pages 46–47
1. c    2. d    3. a
4. True.
5. c    6. b    7. b
8. b    9. a    10. c
11. **False.** Pikachu was the star of the Pokémon video games.
12. c    13. c

## There's an App for That, pages 48–49
1. b    2. d    3. a    4. d
5. **False.** But he does visit the Middle Ages, the Renaissance, a pirate ship, ancient Egypt, ancient Greece, the Stone Age, and the disco era.
6. a    7. c    8. a
9. b    10. b
11. True.    12. a

## Monster Mash, pages 50–51
1. b
2. **False.** He actually lives underwater.
3. a    4. b    5. a
6. b    7. c
8. **True.** The idea of Frankenstein being brought to life by lightning is often shown in movies, but the book's author, Mary Shelley, never provides an explanation.
9. a    10. b    11. c
12. b    13. a

## True or False? Blockbuster Books, pages 52–53
1. **False.** *Journey to the Center of the Earth* was written by Jules Verne; H. G. Wells wrote *The Time Machine*.
2. **False.** The story takes place in the Swiss Alps.
3. **True.** James's parents are eaten by a rhinoceros, even though rhinoceroses are actually plant-eaters.
4. **False.** Pippi Longstocking wears her hair in pigtails.
5. **False.** In *The Little Prince*, an airplane pilot crashes in the Sahara, where he meets the little prince.
6. **True.** Artemis Fowl kidnaps a fairy and holds her ransom for gold.
7. **False.** *The Maze of Bones* is the first book of the 39 Clues series.
8. **False.** Mrs. Frisby is a field mouse.
9. **True.** Nick refers to pens as frindles to annoy his teacher.
10. **True.** Mr. Krupp, the school principal, turns into Captain Underpants after being hypnotized by a ring.
11. **False.** Peter's younger annoying sibling is his brother, Fudge.
12. **True.** The book is the actual diary of a young Jewish girl who was forced to hide from the Nazis during World War II.
13. **True.** They discover a mermaid whose name is Aquamarine.
14. **False:** The pancake house threatens to destroy a colony of burrowing owls.
15. **True.** Maurice "Mo" Folchart brings characters to life when he reads books aloud.
16. **False.** Stanley's nickname is Caveman. The nickname is given to him by a boy named X-ray.
17. **False.** Dictionopolis is a land of words. Digitopolis is a land of numbers.
18. **True.** When he was a child, Peeta gave Katniss two burned loaves of bread from the bakery, which she used to feed her family.
19. **False.** The half-blood heroes battle the Titans.
20. **True.** The jeans, purchased at a thrift shop, fit all four best friends in the book.
21. **False.** Violet's special skill is chewing gum.
22. **True.** Shiloh is a young beagle that is rescued from its abusive owner by a boy named Marty.

23. **True.** Opal names a stray dog Winn-Dixie after the supermarket where she found him.
24. **False.** Piglet constantly says "Oh, dear" throughout the book.
25. **True.** As the children play Jumanji, the events described in the game start to happen in their home.
26. **True.** The Poppers have the refrigerator remodeled to suit the penguin's needs.
27. **False.** Mary survives an outbreak of cholera.
28. **True.** Charlotte the spider befriends Wilbur and saves him from being killed.
29. **False.** Billy eats worms as part of a bet.
30. **False.** Harry Potter has a scar in the shape of a lightning bolt.

## ANSWERS

## Tune In, pages 54–55
1. d    2. b    3. c    4. c
5. b    6. c    7. a
8. True.
9. c    10. a    11. a    12. b
13. b

## True or False? Ready, Set, Action! pages 56–57
1. **False.** The movie takes place in London's British Museum.
2. **False.** Emma Watson played Hermione Granger in the Harry Potter series. Bella Swan was played by Kristen Stewart.
3. **True.** In the movie *Maleficent*, it is revealed that she had her wings cut off.
4. **True.** The rat, named Buddy, resides in Liberty Park with Surly.
5. **True.** The kids discover the alien after receiving a series of strange signals on their phones.
6. **False.** The dolphin's name is Winter.
7. **False.** Thor is a god. However, Captain America did get his powers by taking part in a military experiment.
8. **False.** Vikings live on the island of Berk.
9. **False.** Batman joins forces with Superman, Wonder Woman, and Green Lantern.
10. **False.** E.T. eats Reese's Pieces.
11. **False.** The movie shows his father, Anakin Skywalker, as a young boy.
12. **False.** The turtles love to eat pizza.
13. **True.** The machine is Mr. Peabody's invention.
14. **False.** Hermey wants to be a dentist.
15. **False.** Steve Rogers is the alias of Captain America. Bruce Wayne is Batman.
16. **True.** A powerful lawn mower called the Terrafirminator goes out of control and nearly destroys the gardens.
17. **True.** Mumble cannot sing, but he can tap dance.
18. **False.** He must protect the city from Lord Shen, a peacock.
19. **True.** The two live in a city made of plastic, so a tree is a rare thing.
20. **True.** The witch shouts, "I'm melting" as she disintegrates.
21. **False.** Marlin is a clownfish.
22. **True.** The kids, who call themselves "The Goonies," discover a map to a treasure inside a cavern.
23. **True.** Against all odds, Remy decides to pursue his dream after ending up in the sewers of Paris.

24. **True.** All the characters crave water in this desert setting.
25. **False.** Shrek makes a deal with Rumpelstiltskin.
26. **True.** Norman can speak to the dead, but no one except his friend, Neil, believes him.
27. **False.** According to Buddy, believing in Santa will make his sleigh fly.
28. **True.** The machine, which stands for Flint Lockwood Diatonic Super Mutating Dynamic Food Replicator, was also responsible for creating the meatball storm in the first movie of the series.

29. **True.** President Snow changes the rules of the games. The 75th anniversary of the Hunger Games is called a Quarter Quell, with special rules.
30. **True.** Cade discovers the Autobot truck in an old movie theater.

## Game Show: Ultimate Pop Culture Challenge, pages 58–59

1. d   2. b   3. b   4. c

5. **d**
6. **False.** However, Molly Brown, Archibald Gracie, Captain Edward John Smith, Thomas Andrews, and Joseph Bruce Ismay were all based on real people.
7. a   8. c   9. c   10. a
11. b   12. b   13. c   14. b

# SCORING

### 0–41
## ROOKIE REPORTER
The occasional video game or blockbuster may be up your alley. Although being up-to-date on hot trends isn't your cup of tea, you don't want friends to think you're stuck in the 1990s.

### 42–83
## STAR POWER
You know who's who in Hollywood from reading tabloid headlines while checking out at the grocery store. But there's still more to find out about books, music, and more.

### 84–125
## POP ICON
You give Taylor Swift a run for her money! You rock out to the Top 40 and catch every flick's opening weekend. You top the charts with your pop culture knowledge.

# Get OUTSIDE

## Seasons of Change, pages 62–63

1. **a.** For example, when the Northern Hemisphere is tilted toward the sun summer occurs there; when it is tilted away from the sun, winter occurs.
2. **b**
3. **a.** In the Southern Hemisphere, seasons are the reverse of those in the Northern Hemisphere.
4. b   5. d
6. **False.** Raccoons spend more time in their dens during the winter, but don't hibernate.
7. c   8. c   9. a
10. b   11. d   12. c

## Storm Central, pages 64–65

1. c   2. c   3. a   4. d
5. **True.** Wind chill—a combination of wind and low temperature—is the loss of heat from living things.
6. **False.** A waterspout can lift fish or frogs from water and drop them over land, causing a rain of fish or frogs!
7. a   8. c   9. b

10. **True.** First, an invisible negative charge hits Earth, and then a bright flash goes back up.
11. a   12. b
13. **b.** The dust comes from the Sahara and is carried in clouds. It then falls with the rain over Europe.
14. **False.** The temperature in the clouds where the snow forms must be freezing, but the temperature at ground level can be as high as 40°F (4.4°C).

## Great Gardens, pages 66–67

1. c   2. a
3. **False.** Many cactuses bloom with colorful flowers.
4. c
5. **True.** Zen gardens contain carefully placed rocks and sand raked into patterns.
6. d
7. **False.** The rose garden also includes tulips, daffodils, and more.
8. b   9. a   10. c   11. a

## Rolling Down River, pages 68–69

1. a   2. c
3. **True.** People use up all of the river water before it can reach the sea.
4. d   5. c
6. **False.** The coxswain—who doesn't row—keeps the boat on course and calls out instructions.
7. a   8. d   9. b
10. b   11. c   12. a
13. **False.** The Nile River is natural. Ancient Egyptians relied on its yearly floods to water crops.
14. c   15. b

## Rockin' Redwoods, pages 70–71

1. **True.** As the climate changed, many redwood species went extinct.
2. c   3. c
4. **b.** The General Sherman is the biggest tree in the world by total trunk volume.
5. d   6. a   7. b
8. **False.** A tree in Yosemite National Park used to have a tunnel, but the tree fell in a storm.
9. a
10. **False.** Redwood trees in parks are protected, but trees on private land may be cut.
11. c   12. d

**ANSWERS**

13. **c.** Redwood needles can absorb water from fog and send it down the trunk.
14. **True.** Giant sequoias have fire-resistant bark.

## Cool Caves, pages 72–73

1. c    2. a    3. c
4. b    5. d    6. b
7. **False.** Some bats hunt during the day and sleep at night in trees.
8. b    9. b
10. **True.** Oil from your skin keeps water from dripping down and growing the formation.
11. a    12. d    13. d
14. **True.** There's not much to see in the depths of a dark cave!

## Map Mania! Nature Made, pages 74–75

1. a    2. c    3. b
4. d    5. a    6. c
7. **E.** Ayers Rock
8. **F.** Cave of Crystals
9. **A.** Uyuni Salt Flats
10. **C.** Cotton Palace, Pamukkale
11. **B.** Red Beach
12. **D.** The Wave

## True or False? Life Zones, pages 76–77

1. **False.** Polar bears live in the Arctic.
2. **True.** Many fish and jellyfish have transparent bodies.
3. **True.** In most of Alaska, the sun is up for 20 or more hours a day in the summer.
4. **True.** Ostriches have great eyesight and zebras have a great sense of smell, so together they can detect predators more easily.
5. **False.** Flamingos are born white and only turn pink if they eat a certain diet.

6. **False.** Cattle egrets eat insects, often off the backs of cows and other large animals.
7. **True.** Clownfish have a special coating on their skin that protects them.
8. **False.** Sagebrush grows on the grasslands of North America.
9. **False.** Viruses can't reproduce on their own, so are not considered to be alive.
10. **True.** Earth was much warmer during the Eocene period 53 million years ago.
11. **True.** The fish remove parasites from the sharks.
12. **False.** Anacondas live in the rain forests of South America.
13. **True.** The frozen ground is called permafrost.
14. **False.** Cattails are a freshwater plant.
15. **True.** A species of alga lives inside most coral polyps.
16. **True.** The stand is actually one living thing, all connected by the same roots.
17. **False.** Caribou live in northern parts of North America, Europe, and Asia.
18. **True.** Fleas, tapeworms, and barnacles are all parasites.
19. **False.** Jackals live in Africa, Europe, and Asia, whereas coyotes live in North America.
20. **True.** The mangroves reduce the height and speed of water surging onto land.
21. **False.** In a symbiotic relationship, one or both creatures get some benefit.
22. **False.** Spiny lobsters live in tropical waters.
23. **False.** Large shrimplike creatures and sea cucumbers live there.
24. **True.** Antarctic soil is just sand and small rocks, but penguin poop contains nutrients.
25. **True.** Paleontologists have discovered dinosaur eggs, skulls, and other bones.
26. **False.** The conditions at the summits of many tall mountains are too cold and harsh for trees to grow.
27. **True.** Sharks can sense electric fields and likely confuse the cables with fish.
28. **True.** The pink Amazon River dolphin is one of four freshwater dolphin species.

29. **True.** These bacteria help digest the food you eat.
30. **False.** Kangaroos eat plants.

## The Sandy Sahara, pages 78–79

1. a    2. d    3. b
4. **False.** The saguaro only grows in the deserts of North America.
5. a    6. d    7. c    8. d
9. **True.** The reserve protects desert species such as the addax and desert cheetah.
10. a    11. c
12. **True.** The eyelashes help protect a camel's eyes from blowing sand.

## Game Show: Ultimate Nature Challenge, pages 80–81

1. **True.** White-tailed deer and sheep can also eat poison ivy.
2. c    3. a
4. **True.** These super dry regions contain no plants or wildlife.
5. d    6. a    7. b
8. **False.** Pink grasshoppers are rare, but they do exist!
9. d    10. a    11. a    12. d
13. d    14. b    15. c

# SCORING

## 0–49
### SUNNY AND CLEAR
You have a bright and cheerful personality that helps you make friends easily. But when it starts to rain, you dash inside. Next time, head outside and splash in some puddles—the more time you spend in nature, the more you'll learn!

## 50–99
### BRAINSTORMER
You aren't at all afraid to get a little wet or muddy, and your mind is constantly spinning with ideas. Start jotting down your brainstorms and looking up answers to your questions, and you could be a great weather forecaster someday.

## 100–149
### HURRICANE WARNING!
When you walk into a room, everyone had better watch out! Like a tropical storm, you'll spin circles around the smartest person there. You know updrafts, downdrafts, and supercells. Someday, you'll probably be a famous inventor or storm chaser.

# Picture the PAST

## It's Greek to Me, pages 84–85

1. **b**
2. **False.** Romans wore togas, whereas Greeks wore tunics called chitons.
3. **c**     4. **a**
5. **False.** The Phoenicians, whose civilization was centered around modern-day Libya and Syria, have that honor. But the Greeks were the first to have symbols for vowels in addition to consonants.
6. **b**     7. **a**     8. **d**     9. **b**
10. **d**     11. **b**
12. **True.**

## True or False? History's Headlines, pages 86–87

1. **False.** The day was called Black Tuesday.
2. **True.**    3. **True.**    4. **True.**
5. **False.** The plague came to Europe in "death ships" full of sick and dying crew members that landed at Messina, Sicily.
6. **False.** January 1, 1863, occurred in the middle of the war and freed the slaves living in the Confederate states of the southern United States.
7. **False.** About 700 people were rescued from the wreckage.
8. **False.** Michelangelo painted the chapel.
9. **False.** It united East and West Germany.
10. **False.** He rose to power at age nine.
11. **True.**
12. **False.** The first mass-produced book was the Bible.
13. **True.**
14. **True.**
15. **False.** Pompeii was destroyed by the eruption of Mount Vesuvius.
16. **True.**
17. **False.** He actually left August 3, 1492, making the trip a total of two months, nine days.
18. **False.** He formed the People's Republic of China, which was a communist government.
19. **False.** He delivered it in Washington, D.C.
20. **True.**
21. **False.** The ancestor was *Homo habilis*, a precursor to *Homo erectus*.
22. **False.** Jacqueline Kennedy did not die.
23. **True.**
24. **True.**
25. **True.**
26. **True.**

27. **False.** President F. W. de Klerk and his government ended apartheid, or racial segregation. Nelson Mandela was elected the country's first black president in 1994.
28. **False.** Magnavox made the Odyssey.
29. **True.**
30. **False.** Sir Edmund Hillary was from New Zealand.

## Map Mania! Dig This, pages 88–89

1. **a**    2. **c**    3. **b**    4. **b**
5. **d**    6. **a**
7 **C.** Nasca, Peru
8. **D.** Leicester, U.K.
9. **F.** Xi'an, China
10. **E.** Mesa Verde National Park, U.S.A.
11. **B.** Afar Desert, Ethiopia
12. **A.** Rosetta, Egypt

## Show Stoppers, pages 90–91

1. **c**      2. **a**
3. **False.** Historians have recorded battles of female gladiators, and in 2000 historians found the grave of a female gladiator near London.
4. **a**      5. **d**      6. **a**
7. **False.** Hieroglyphics of jugglers have been found in ancient Egyptian tombs.
8. **d**      9. **c**      10. **b**
11. **True.**    12. **a**

## Girl Power, pages 92–93

1. **b**     2. **True.**     3. **a**
4. **b**     5. **d**
6. **True.** She's also the only woman to win two Nobel Prizes: for physics in 1903 and for chemistry in 1911.
7. **a**      8. **d**
9. **b.** For her pioneering work, Malala Yousafzai was awarded the Nobel Peace Prize in 2014.
10. **a**
11. **False.** She led the troops to victory at Orléans.
12. **d**

## The Secrets of Easter Island, pages 94–95

1. **d**     2. **d**
3. **False.** Although the heads are larger than normal, they all have bodies buried underground. Over time, soil erosion has buried the bodies.

4. **a**    5. **d**    6. **a**   7. **a**      8. **b**
9. **True.** It is still not fully certain how the islanders moved the statues, each of which had an average weight of 14 tons (12,700 kg).
10. **c**
11. **True.** Archaeologists think that they represent the spirits of ancestors, chiefs, or other important figures. But there is no written record.
12. **d**

## The Royal Treatment, pages 96–97

1. **a**     2. **a**     3. **b**
4. **d**     5. **c**     6. **b**
7. **True.** He won the horse when he was 12 and rode it into battle for many years.
8. **a**    9. **d**    10. **d**    11. **d**
12. **a**

## Battle Zones, pages 98–99

1. **c**     2. **a**     3. **b**     4. **a**
5. **True.**    6. **d**    7. **c**
8. **d**     9. **c**     10. **b**

## Game Show: Ultimate History Challenge, pages 100–101

1. **c**
2. **False.** They lived in a cloud palace above the mountain.
3. **c**    4. **a**    5. **a**    6. **a**
7. **d**    8. **b**    9. **True.** 10. **d**
11. **c**    12. **a**    13. **a**    14. **True.**

# SCORING

## 0–42

### MODERN MARVEL
You know all about the here and now, but need to bone up on the past. Go check out a museum or historical landmark. You may find out that you are more of a history buff than you think you are.

## 43–85

### TIME TRAVELER
It's not all Greek to you. From Napoleon to Alexander the Great, you know your historical figures—though you could take some time to dig deeper into the past.

## 86–126

### BLAST FROM THE PAST!
You would fit right in at King Henry's court. You've got a great grasp of important events in history—everything from the fall of the Roman Empire to the sinking of the *Titanic*.

# Go FIGURE!

## It's a Numbers Game, pages 104–105
1. c    2. b    3. b    4. b
5. **True.** Wilt was playing for the Philadelphia Warriors in a basketball game against the New York Knicks.
6. b    7. c
8. **False.** He became the tallest boxing champion.
9. a    10. c    11. b
12. **False.** Some lacrosse games are also three periods long.
13. b

## Taj Mahal, pages 106–107
1. b    2. b    3. c
4. **True.** They carried the heavy materials to the site.
5. a    6. c    7. c
8. **False.** It is closed on Friday, not Sunday.
9. c    10. a    11. b    12. c
13. **True.** This is known as the structure's reverberation time.

## Pay Day! pages 108–109
1. b    2. c    3. b
4. **False.** It was boxer Floyd Mayweather, who earned $105,000,000.
5. a
6. **False.** It is believed to be baseball pitcher Nolan Ryan, who signed the record contract before the 1980 season.

7. c    8. a    9. a
10. **True.** It was the second year in a row at the top spot for Downey, who also earned $75 million in 2013.

## Map Mania! How Many People? pages 110–111
1. a    2. c    3. b    4. c
5. a    6. b
7. India, C    8. Vatican City, F
9. **South Africa, D**    10. Iceland, B
11. Inca Empire, E    12. Antarctica, A

## Go the Distance, pages 112–113
1. b    2. c    3. a
4. **False.** In 1999, Bertrand Piccard (Switzerland) and Brian Jones (U.K.) set the record with a flight of 25,361 miles (40,815 km), which is a little more than once around the globe.

5. a    6. b    7. c
8. **True.** At the 2014 World Cup, the fields (known as the "pitch") were 115 yards (105 m) long.
9. b    10. a    11. c
12. **True.** It was thrown by former college football quarterback Joe Ayoob.

## True or False? One to Thirty, pages 114–115
1. **False.** It's a Cyclops.
2. **True.** Its scientific name is *Adalia bipunctata*.
3. **True.** The coin was helpful at the time for buying stamps.
4. **False.** It opens in the late afternoon.
5. **True.** But his seven daughters all have different names.
6. **False.** They are found only in southern Africa.
7. **True.** It was released on February 4, 1938.
8. **False.** It is sometimes called solids and stripes, or spots and stripes, or high-low.
9. **False.** They demoted Pluto to a dwarf planet, leaving us with eight official planets.
10. **True.** Each place value is 10 times the one to its right.

11. **False.** The name came about because for years the stores opened at 7 a.m. and closed at 11 p.m.

12. **True.** It was an increase of 7.7 percent from 2012.

13. **False.** Arithmophobia is a general fear of numbers. The word for fear of the number 13 is "triskaidekaphobia."

14. **False.** This kind of poem is called a sonnet.

15. **True.** The second point is indicated by 30 and the third is 40.

16. **True.** There are one king, one queen, two rooks, two bishops, two knights, and eight pawns.

17. **False.** The day is May 17.

18. **True.** Argon is a noble gas in the far right column of the Periodic Table.

19. **True.** The total number is 20,000 to 25,000.

20. **True.** They are numbered 1 to 20, and the large part of each section is worth that number of points.

21. **True.** You must be a citizen for 20 years—and not be a member of the military or police.

22. **True.** And Hebrew is written from right to left.

23. **False.** It meant "go away."

24. **False.** It was the Egyptians.

25. **True.** In the United States, the game is known as Parcheesi.

26. **True.** There are also 33 joints and more than 100 tendons, muscles, and ligaments.

27. **False.** It's known as a perfect game.

28. **False.** There are 28 tiles in the entire set.

29. **True.** It takes Uranus 84 years, and Neptune almost 165 years.

30. **True.** They completed it on New Year's Eve.

## Off the Scale, pages 116–117

1. **True.** It was invented in 1742 by the Swedish astronomer Anders Celsius.
2. c
3. **False.** It goes from 0 to 12.
4. a     5. c     6. b     7. b
8. **True.** That system was "sexagesimal"—counting in 60s.
9. a     10. c     11. c
12. **True.** It is known as the Julian calendar, which was replaced by the modern Gregorian calendar (12 months with 365 total days) starting in 1582.

## Game Show: Ultimate Number Challenge, pages 118–119

1. d     2. a     3. b
4. **True.** Africa's 2014 population of 1.2 billion people is set to grow to 4 billion.
5. c     6. b
7. **False.** The SPF number indicates how many times longer than your normal burning time you can stay out.
8. b
9. **False.** Supposedly, it was the 19th product Kellogg's developed that year.
10. b
11. **False.** It was Sandra Bullock, star of *Gravity*, who was the top earner, with $51 million.
12. **False.** The land, including the gardens, covers 42 acres (17 ha), or 32 football fields.
13. c     14. b     15. c

# SCORING

## 0–39

### NUMBER NOVICE
You can add 2 plus 2, but when it comes to more complicated calculations, you shy away. Face your fear of numbers, and you'll be ready to tackle trigonometry.

## 40–79

### COOL CALCULATOR
From times tables to the quadratic formula, you're a math whiz. Your good number sense will help you take on the world.

## 80–117

### MATH MAVEN
You know how to crunch your numbers—whether it's the first 100 digits of pi or the square root of 625. Mathematicians Euclid and Pythagoras have nothing on you!

# Super SCIENCE

## Inspired by Nature, pages 122–123

1. b     2. d     3. b     4. a
5. **False.** While many such numbers do follow patterns, there are no mathematical rules governing nature.

6. a     7. d     8. c     9. d
10. d     11. c     12. b

## Simple Machines, pages 124–125

1. a     2. d     3. a     4. c
5. **True.** However, the more pulleys you add, the longer it takes to lift the load.
6. a     7. d     8. c
9. **True.** A wheelbarrow combines a wheel and axle and a lever.
10. c     11. a
12. **False.** Don't forget the steering wheel! The engine also contains wheel systems.
13. d     14. b

## Super Star, pages 126–127

1. c
2. d. The number is constantly changing as sunspots disappear and reappear.
3. **False.** The sun orbits around the center of the Milky Way galaxy.
4. a     5. b     6. d     7. a
8. **True.** SOHO, the Solar and Heliospheric Observatory, has been in operation monitoring the sun since 1995.
9. c     10. c     11. b     12. b
13. **True.** The sun's mass is about 330,000 times that of Earth.

## Map Mania!, Animal Rescue!
### pages 128–129
1. d    2. a    3. c    4. c
5. b    6. c
7. Pelicans, F    8. Elephants, A
9. Sea turtles, C    10. Sharks, D
11. Parrots, E
12. Kangaroos, B

## True or False? Eureka!
### pages 130–131
1. **False.** Albert Einstein wrote this equation, which defines the conservational relationship between mass and energy.
2. **False.** The first paper was invented in China between 140 and 86 B.C.
3. **False.** The 1948 book *Your Creative Power*, by Alex Osborn, coined the word "brainstorm."
4. **True.** The first iPod could hold about 1,000 songs.
5. **False.** The stone statues are on Easter Island.
6. **False.** The first Russian space rockets were called Soyuz.
7. **True.** Dean Kamen invented the Segway.
8. **True.** The pigeons are now part of the Natural History Museum in London.
9. **False.** "Eureka" is Greek for "I've found it."
10. **False.** The first call from a mobile phone was made in 1973.
11. **True.** Louis Daguerre developed the daguerreotype process in 1839.
12. **False.** The concept of the number zero arose more than a thousand years ago.
13. **True.** The two fought over which type of electrical current was best: AC or DC.
14. **True.** Percy Spencer noticed that when he stood near a magnetron, a candy bar in his pocket melted!
15. **True.** Galileo invented an improved telescope that let him see some of the moons. More have been seen since then.
16. **True.** Loewi showed that the brain transmits information with chemicals.
17. **True.** A single pack of early matches contained enough toxins to kill a person.
18. **False.** Marie Curie studied radioactivity. She won the Nobel Prize twice, in 1903 for physics and in 1911 for chemistry.

19. **True.** The melon produced a strain of the earliest antibiotic: penicillin.
20. **False.** Benjamin Franklin did perform experiments during thunderstorms and invented the lightning rod.
21. **True.** Kids loved to play with the squishy dough, so the company took out the cleaning chemicals and added colors.
22. **True.** Gunpowder (and fireworks) were developed in China between A.D. 960–1279.
23. **False.** Copernicus was a famous astronomer who proposed that the planets all orbit the sun.
24. **True.** On the Apollo 17 mission, Gene Cernan taped a broken fender together.
25. **False.** The Roomba is a robot vacuum cleaner.
26. **True.** The assembly line began rolling on December 1, 1913.
27. **True.** The device got the name "flashlight" because of these short flashes of light.
28. **False.** The original idea for the name was Twttr, which became Twitter.
29. **True.** Dolly the sheep was cloned in 1997.
30. **False.** The first e-books launched in 1998, and the Kindle came out in 2007.

## Cretaceous Giants,
### pages 132–133
1. b    2. d    3. a
4. c
5. **False.** The *Plesiosaur*, a giant that lived in the sea, gave birth to live young.
6. d    7. a
8. **False.** This dinosaur is often called *Brontosaurus* but its official name is *Apatosaurus*.
9. c    10. d
11. **True.** During this warm period in Earth's history, there were no ice caps.
12. d    13. c

## Nosing Around,
### pages 134–135
1. c    2. a    3. c    4. b    5. a
6. **True.** The rats wear harnesses, and scratch the ground when they find a bomb.
7. b    8. c    9. d    10. d
11. **True.** A dog's sense of smell is 10,000 to 100,000 times stronger than a human's.
12. a
13. **False.** The tapir and the elephant seal have short trunks.

## It's Elemental,
### pages 136–137
1. c    2. a    3. d
4. a. Copper reacts with oxygen and turns to green copper oxide.
5. b
6. **False.** Red-orange signs likely contain neon, but other colors come from different elements or fluorescent lighting.
7. c    8. b    9. d
10. d    11. b
12. **False.** Many of the elements with high numbers have been created only in a lab.
13. a
14. **True.** The famous composer drank from a goblet made of lead.

## Game Show: Ultimate Science Challenge,
### pages 138–139
1. b
2. **True.** The bearcat, or binturong, is native to southeast Asia.
3. **False.** The *Tyrannosaurus rex* walked with its back and tail parallel to the ground.
4. c    5. a    6. b.
7. b    8. d
9. **False.** The device got the name "mouse" because it looked like one.
10. c    11. d    12. a
13. b    14. d    15. c

# SCORING

### 0–45
## ROOKIE RESEARCHER
You're likely new to science, which means that you make more mistakes than a pro. But don't lose heart—many great inventions happened by accident. Keep going and you could be famous someday!

### 46–91
## MAD SCIENTIST
You know everything there is to know about one thing, whether it's outer space or car engines or dinosaurs. Obsessions can lead to discoveries, but it's also a good idea to broaden your horizons and try something new.

### 92–136
## FAMOUS INVENTOR
We bet you've said "Eureka!" more than once in your life. Great ideas come to you easily, and you always remember facts and figures. Put your skills to work as an inventor, and someday you'll change the world!

## Adventure QUEST

### To the Rescue!
### pages 142–143
1. **True.** The letters, which were first used as a distress signal in the early 1900s, were chosen because they are easy to type in Morse code.
2. **c**          3. **c**
4. **True.** K-9 is a homophone of canine.
5. **c**     6. **d**     7. **c**
8. **a**     9. **a**     10. **b**
11. **c.** Polaris is better known by its nickname, the North Star.
12. **True.** Salt water is toxic to humans. The large amount of salt it contains is difficult for humans to expel from their bodies.
13. **a**
14. **False.** Dalmatians were used because, upon hearing a fire bell, they would sprint out in front of a firehouse to alert that a fire truck would be pulling out. Also, during the time of horse-drawn carriages, they were a calming presence to horses, which fear fire.

### True or False?
### Parks of the World,
### pages 144–145
1. **True.** The cave, which is located in Carlsbad Caverns National Park in New Mexico, U.S.A., is 1,604 feet (489 m) deep, whereas the Empire State Building measures 1,454 feet (443 m) from base to the top of the antenna.
2. **False.** The world's tallest known tree, called Hyperion, is located in Redwood National Park, California, U.S.A. It stands 379.1 feet (115.6 m) tall.
3. **True.** Ruins of Maya palaces, temples, and public squares can be found in the park.
4. **True.** The rock was shaped by water erosion over millions of years.
5. **True.** In the 1860s the park was developed in response to San Francisco's growing population. New businesses transformed San Francisco into a booming—and crowded—city.
6. **False.** The country's first national park was Yellowstone National Park, which was established by Ulysses S. Grant.
7. **True.** The geyser got its name because it faithfully spouts every 63–70 minutes.
8. **False.** Olympic National Park is named after the peninsula on which it is located.
9. **True.** It hit 134°F (57°C) on July 10, 1913.
10. **True.** The park is home to Mount Logan, which stands 19,550 feet (5,959 m) tall.
11. **True.** Mount Aso is located in Aso Kuju National Park. The volcano's caldera measures about 23 miles (37 km) in diameter.
12. **True.** Angel Falls measures 3,212 feet (979 m) tall. The world's tallest building—Burj Khalifa—measures 2,716 feet (828 m) from base to tip.
13. **False.** The blue-footed booby can be found in Galápagos National Park in Ecuador, as well as in other parks along the Pacific Coast of the Americas.
14. **True.** Denali National Park and Preserve covers 9,492 square miles (24,584 sq km) whereas the state of New Hampshire spans 9,350 square miles (24,216 sq km).
15. **True.** The wildebeest migrate to the Serengeti from November to April for food and water.
16. **True.** The Grand Canyon, located in Arizona, U.S.A., was carved out over millions of years by the Colorado River.
17. **True.** Since 2007, 20 have been established around the world.
18. **True.** More than 120,000 Magellanic penguins visit the

island every year to breed.

19. **True.** It was formed in 1932 by joining Glacier National Park in the United States with Waterton Lakes National Park in Canada.
20. **False.** The Statue of Liberty National Monument is part of the U.S. National Park Service, but it is not a national park.
21. **False.** The park is home to the Aboriginal people. The Cherokee Indians live in the United States.
22. **True.** Northeast Greenland National Park measures a whopping 603,972 square miles (1,564,280 sq km). By comparison, Italy spans 116,345 square miles (301,332 sq km).
23. **False.** The name refers to the mammoth size of the cave.
24. **True.** The mountain is located in Sagarmatha National Park in Nepal.
25. **True.** Many dinosaur fossils have been found in Talampaya National Park in Argentina.
26. **False.** Delaware is the only state that does not have an area administered by the National Park Service.
27. **False.** Although Banff is home to the woodland caribou, there is no record of it—or any other species of caribou flying. This is a joke question!
28. **True.** Zhangjiajie National Forest park in China's Hunan Province has many sandstone cliffs and quartz cliffs that inspired the world of Pandora.
29. **False.** Fjords are narrow inlets of the sea between high cliffs.
30. **False.** Neither male nor female Tsavo lions have proper manes.

## Spy School, pages 146–147

| | | | |
|---|---|---|---|
| 1. b | 2. c | 3. b | 4. b |
| 5. d | 6. c | 7. a | 8. a |
| 9. a | 10. c | 11. c | |

12. **True.** High-resolution satellites are able to pick up small details such as newspaper headlines.
13. a

## Tomb Raider, pages 148–149

1. **b.** Scarab beetles were important symbols, representing rebirth to the Egyptians.

| 2. c | 3. d | 4. a | 5. a |
|---|---|---|---|

6. **True.** The ancient Egyptians believed that they could continue to live in the afterlife, so they had their most useful possessions packed in their tombs.

| 7. b | 8. **True.** |
|---|---|
| 9. a | 10. a |

11. **False.** Ibises are a type of bird associated with Thoth—god of wisdom, magic, and measurement—and were often featured on the tombs.
12. **a.** They left the heart, believing it was the center of a person's being and intelligence.

| 13. d | 14. d |
|---|---|

## The Adventures of Marco Polo, pages 150–151

| 1. b | 2. a | 3. a |
|---|---|---|
| 4. c | 5. b | |

6. **False.** Many Europeans ventured to China, including Alexander the Great and the Greek explorer Skylax.

| 7. a | 8. a | 9. c |
|---|---|---|
| 10. d | 11. b | 12. d |

13. **False.** Just a few decades after Polo's journey, a Moroccan explorer named Ibn Battuta traveled 73,000 miles (117,482 km). That's about three times the distance covered by Polo. In modern times, many people have flown farther than this.

## The Everglades, pages 152–153

| 1. a | 2. a | 3. c |
|---|---|---|
| 4. c | 5. a | 6. c |

7. **True.** The two animals live in the same region and are the only crocodilian species native to the United States.

| 8. a | 9. d | 10. c |
|---|---|---|
| 11. b | 12. a | |

13. **False.** The Everglades receive little to no rainfall from December to April.

## Map Mania!, Celebrate Outdoors, pages 154–155

| 1. d | 2. b | 3. a | 4. a |
|---|---|---|---|
| 5. b | 6. c | 7. a | 8. 1D |
| 9. 2A | 10. 3C | 11. 4F | |
| 12. 5E | 13. 6B | 14. 7G | |

9. c          10. a
11. **False.** Marco was joined by his father,
    Niccolo, and his uncle, Maffeo.
12. b          13. b          14. a

# SCORING

## 0–41

### AT THE TRAILHEAD
It may be daunting to set out on an adventure. But there's lots to learn by trying new things. Go for a hike or take a snowboarding lesson. You never know how adventurous you are until you try.

## 42–83

### MID-MOUNTAIN STOP
You have no problem hitting the trails, but you may stall out before reaching the end. Keep up the good work, and you'll make it to your goal.

## 84–125

### PEAK EXPLORER
You don't need to send an SOS. You're ready for another adventure. So strap on your boots, and get ready to scale every mountain peak.

# GRAND TALLY

Did your brain get a good workout with *Quiz Whiz 6*? Will it be sore tomorrow? Or did it barely break a sweat? Tally up your totals from all eight chapters to see how your score shows off your brainpower.

## 0–342

### TRIVIA NOVICE
You may be new to the trivia game, but you're not going to give up on learning new things. These questions are just the jumping-off point for you to find out more. Hit the books, scour the Internet, and read up on current events. Pretty soon you'll be quizzing your friends and family to help them train *their* brains.

## 343–685

### APPRENTICE
Factoids, figures, and fun tidbits are your thing. You have a head start on becoming a Quiz Whiz. Just start digging a little deeper into subjects you haven't had the time to study yet, and you'll be on your way to mastery.

## 686–1,028

### THE WHIZ OF QUIZ
What a workout! Your brain is in peak condition. You already have a well-rounded mix of knowledge, and you're ready to take it to the next level!

## Photo Credits

Credit key: CI–Corbis Images; DRMS–Dreamstime; GI–Getty Images; IS–iStock; REX–Rex Features; RH–Robert Harding; SPL–SPL; SS–Shutterstock; TF–Topfoto

### Cover
(UP LE), B.S.P.I./CI; (UP RT), Elena Shashkina/SS; (CTR LE), filmfoto/SS; (LO LE), Vitaly Titov & Maria Sidelnikova/SS; (LO RT), Image Broker/RH; BackCover: (UP), Photographerlondon/DRMS; (LO), The Granger Collection/TF; (Spine), Vitaly Titov & Maria Sidelnikova/SS

### Front Matter
1 (UP), B.S.P.I./CI; 1 (LO), Vitaly Titov & Maria Sidelnikov/SS; 3 (CTR LE), filmfoto/SS; 4 (UP LE), Protea/DRMS; 4 (LO RT), Gleb Tarro/SS; 4 (LO LE), Fedor Selivanov/SS; 4 (UP RT), TF; 5 (UP LE), Matyas Rehak/SS; 5 (UP RT), Volt Collection/SS; 5 (LO RT), Vitalii Nesterchuk/SS; 5 (LO LE), Piotr Pawinski/DRMS; 6 (LO), WilleeCole Photography/SS

### In the Wild [8–25]
8-9 (BACKGROUND), Protea/DRMS; 10-11 (BACKGROUND), Willyam Bradberry/SS; 12 (CTR), Amichaelbrown/DRMS; 12 (LO), Anan Chincho/DRMS; 12 (UP), Ondrej Prosicky/SS; 13 (UP), Sombra12/DRMS; 13 (LO), Tracey King/DRMS; 14-15 (BACKGROUND), Ethan Daniels/SS; 16 (CTR), Dule964/DRMS; 16 (LO), Iakov Filimonov/DRMS; 16 (UP), Brian Kushner/DRMS; 17 (LO LE), Atalvi/DRMS; 17 (UP), Iakov Filimonov/DRMS; 17 (LO RT), Anankkml/DRMS; 20 (LO), Dmytro Pylypenko/DRMS; 20 (CTR), Simone Winkler/DRMS; 20 (UP), Mattiasj/DRMS; 21 (CTR), Photographerlondon/DRMS; 21 (UP), Isselee/DRMS; 21 (LO), Afonskaya Irina/DRMS; 22-23 (BACKGROUND), Andraå Cerar/SS; 24 (UP), Vladimir Melnik/DRMS; 24 (CTR), Nahuel Condino/DRMS; 24 (LO), Brian Sedgbeer/DRMS; 25 (UP), Amsis1/DRMS; 25 (CTR LE), Akinshin/DRMS; 25 (LO), Jorg Hackemann/DRMS; 25 (CTR RT), Frans Lanting/RH

### Wild World [26–43]
26-27 (BACKGROUND), Fedor Selivanov/SS; 28 (LO), Nicholas Piccillo/DRMS; 28 (UP), Gulrez Khan/DRMS; 28 (CTR), Debby Wong/SS; 29 (UP), The Asahi Shimbun/GI; 29 (LO), syzx/SS; 29 (CTR), Bill Frakes/GI; 30-31 (BACKGROUND), Olgysha/SS; 34 (UP), Mikel Bilbao/RH; 34 (LO), Eag1e/DRMS; 34 (CTR LE), EQRoy/SS; 34 (CTR RT), HoleInTheBox/SS; 35 (CTR), Frank Fiedler/SS; 35 (UP), Egmont Strigl/RH; 35 (LO), Wolfgang Diederich/RH; 36-37 (BACKGROUND), Nadezda Sereda/SS; 38 (LO), Greenland/DRMS; 38 (UP), D.Shashikant/SS; 39 (UP LE), Kguzel/DRMS; 39 (LO), Liviu Toader/SS; 39 (UP RT), Thinkstock Images/GI; 40 (3), Kennerth Kullman/DRMS; 40 (4), Jsingh1699/DRMS; 40 (5), Hayati Kayhan/DRMS; 40 (2), Lukasz Gajewski/DRMS; 40 (1), Canonphotolife/DRMS; 41 (6), Robyn Mackenzie/DRMS; 41 (7), Alexandr Blinov/DRMS; 41 (8), Aurelio Scetta/DRMS; 41 (9), Billkret/DRMS; 41 (10), Ferenz/DRMS; 41 (11), Junpinzon/DRMS; 42 (LO), minnystock/

DRMS; 42 (UP), Mattiass/DRMS; 43 (LO), Zabiamdeve/DRMS; 43 (CTR), Lightkeeper/DRMS; 43 (UP), cossmix/SS


## Pop Culture [44–59]
44-45 (BACKGROUND), Topfoto; 46 (UP), Carrienelson1/DRMS; 46 (LO), Business Wire/GI; 47 (LO), Igor Terekhov/DRMS; 47 (UP), Featureflash/SS; 48-49 (BACKGROUND), Mikado767/DRMS; 50 (LO), Topham Picturepoint/TF; 50 (UP), c.Warner Br/Everett/REX; 50 (CTR), Michael Gray/DRMS; 51 (UP), World History Archive/TF; 51 (LO), RIA Novosti/TF; 54 (UP), Kenneth D Durden/DRMS; 54 (LO), Kevin Mazur/AMA2014/GI; 55 (UP), Malivoja/DRMS; 55 (LO), TF; 58 (LO), La Fabrika Pixel S.l./DRMS; 58 (CTR), Pavel Losevsky/DRMS; 58 (UP), John Alex Maguire/Rex USA; 59 (UP CTR RT), Sarah2/DRMS; 59 (LO CTR RT), Linqong/DRMS; 59 (LO-A), TF; 59 (LO-B), Topham Picturepoint/TF; 59 (LO-C), ullsteinbild/TF; 59 (LO-D), Paper Boat Creative/GI; 59 (UP), Courtesy Everett Collection/Rex USA; 59 (LO-C), ullsteinbild/TF


## Get Outside [60–81]
60-61 (BACKGROUND), Gleb Tarro/SS; 62 (UP), Santos06/DRMS; 62 (CTR), Jamie Roach/DRMS; 62 (LO), Isselee/DRMS; 63 (UP), Elena Schweitzer/DRMS; 63 (LO), Aquariagirl1970/DRMS; 64-65 (BACKGROUND), solarseven/SS; 66 (LO), Janeykay2007/DRMS; 66 (UP), Fine Art Images/HIP/TF; 67 (UP), Piccia Neri/DRMS; 67 (CTR), Happystock/DRMS; 67 (LO), Suchan/DRMS; 68-69 (BACKGROUND), Vladimir Melnikov/SS; 70-71 (BACKGROUND), Gary Saxe/SS; 72-73 (BACKGROUND), AG-PHOTOS/SS; 74 (UP), Joshua Cortopassi/DRMS; 74 (CTR), P7edch/DRMS; 74 (LO), Carsten Peter/Speleoresearch & Films/GI; 75 (UP), Nikolai Sorokin/DRMS; 75 (CTR), Bcbounders/DRMS; 75 (LO), AFP/Stringer/GI; 78 (UP), Stephane Benito/DRMS; 78 (CTR), Lwroosa/DRMS; 78 (LO), Daniel Boiteau/DRMS; 79 (UP), Eastmanphoto/DRMS; 79 (LO), Matyas Rehak/DRMS; 80 (UP LE), Isselee/DRMS; 80 (UP RT), Iakov Filimonov/DRMS; 80 (LO), Thomas Males/DRMS; 81 (UP LE), Mattwatt/DRMS; 81 (UP-A), Yongsky/DRMS; 81 (UP-B), Christasvengel/DRMS; 81 (UP-C), Yphotoland/DRMS; 81 (UP-D), Wieslaw Jarek/DRMS; 81 (CTR LE), Steve Mann/DRMS; 81 (LO LE), William Perry/DRMS; 81 (LO RT), Steve Byland/DRMS


## Picture the Past [82–101]
82-83 (BACKGROUND), Matyas Rehak/SS; 84-85 (BACKGROUND), Nick Pavlakis/SS; 88 (UP), Jarnogz/DRMS; 88 (LO RT), Steve Allen/DRMS; 88 (LO LE), National Pictures/TF; 89 (UP), Eclecticamusement/DRMS; 89 (LO), Dieter Hawlan/DRMS; 89 (CTR), Julius T Csotoni/SPL; 90 (LO), Juan Moyano/DRMS; 90 (UP), RIA Novosti/TF; 91 (UP), Fine Art Images/Heritage Images/TF; 91 (LO), Nigel Norrington/ArenaPAL/TF; 92 (LO), Topfoto/TF; 94-95 (BACKGROUND), TanArt/SS; 96 (UP), Mocnypunkt/DRMS; 96 (CTR), British Library Board / TF; 96 (LO), The Granger Collection/TF; 97 (UP), The Granger Collection/TF; 97 (LO), World History Archive/TF; 98-99 (BACKGROUND), Colette3/SS; 100 (UP LE), Eleni Seitanidou/DRMS; 100 (LO), Everett Historical/DRMS; 100 (UP RT), Andreasg/DRMS; 101 (CTR LE), Jesse Kraft/DRMS; 101 (UP), Fine Art Images/HIP/TF; 101 (CTR RT), World History Archive/TF; 101 (LO), The Granger Collection/TF

Go Figure! [102–119]
102-103 (BACKGROUND), Piotr Pawinski/DRMS; 104 (UP), Cosmin Iftode/DRMS; 104 (LO), Icon Sports Media/Actionplus/TF; 105 (UP), Bruno Rosa/DRMS; 105 (LO LE), Jean Vaillancourt/DRMS; 105 (LO RT), Walter Arce/DRMS; 106-107 (BACKGROUND), Boris Stroujko/SS; 108 (UP), Patrimonio Designs Limited/DRMS; 108 (LO), Olga Besnard/DRMS; 109 (BACKGROUND), Robertds/DRMS; 109 (UP), Andrey Burmakin/DRMS; 109 (LO), Emanuel Corso/DRMS; 110 (1), Kailash K Soni/DRMS; 110 (2), Gerrit Jan (gj)/DRMS; 110 (3), Hongqi Zhang (aka Michael Zhang)/DRMS; 111 (6), Vladimir Seliverstov/DRMS; 111 (5), Narongsak Nagadhana/DRMS; 111 (4), Sanspek/DRMS; 112 (UP LE), Dwong19/DRMS; 112 (LO), Radu Razvan Gheorghe/DRMS; 112-113 (LO), Olga Kovalenko/DRMS; 112 (UP RT), Monkey Business Images/SS; 113 (UP), Don Emmert/AFP/GI; 116-117 (BACKGROUND), Nordroden/SS; 118 (UP), Pixelrobot/DRMS; 118 (CTR LE), Hamik/DRMS; 118 (CTR RT), Juan Morelis/DRMS; 118 (LO), Joingate/DRMS; 119 (CTR LE), Sergeychernov/DRMS; 119 (CTR RT), Scol22/DRMS; 119 (LO-A), Iakov Filimonov/DRMS; 119 (LO-B), Lilya/DRMS; 119 (LO-C), Yvdavyd/DRMS; 119 (LO-D), IrinaK/SS

Super Science [120-139]
120-121 (BACKGROUND), Volt Collection/SS; 122 (LO LE), Dtvphoto/DRMS; 122 (UP), Stocksnapper/DRMS; 122 (LO RT), Steve Kingsman/DRMS; 123 (CTR), Hans Magelssen/DRMS; 123 (LO), Musat Christian/DRMS; 123 (UP), Cyhel/SS; 124-125 (BACKGROUND), Andrey_Kuzmin/SS; 126-127 (BACKGROUND), silver tiger/SS; 128-129 (UP), R. Gino Santa Maria/Shutterfree, Llc/DRMS; 128 (CTR LE), Mikephotos/DRMS; 128 (CTR RT), Sergio Bertino/SS; 128 (LO), Frans Lanting/RH; 129 (UP), Maxriesgo/DRMS; 129 (LO), Tracey Woods/GI; 132-133 (BACKGROUND), Catmando/SS; 134 (UP), Kjersti Joergensen/DRMS; 134 (LO), Subbotina/DRMS; 134 (CTR), Isselee/DRMS; 135 (LO), Liumangtiger/DRMS; 135 (UP), Ken Catania/Visuals Unlimite, Inc./SPL; 136-137 (BACKGROUND), majcot/SS; 138 (CTR), Cynoclub/DRMS; 138 (LO), Nattul/DRMS; 138 (UP), Leonello Calvetti/DRMS; 139 (UP LE), Sergey Novikov/SS; 139 (UP RT), Felinda/DRMS; 139 (LO RT), Jean-Michel Girard/SS; 139 (LO LE), The Granger Collection/TF

Adventure Quest [140–157]
140-141 (BACKGROUND), Vitalii Nesterchuk/SS; 142 (LO), Dusan Kostic/DRMS; 142 (UP), Idaho Statesman/GettyImages; 143 (UP LE), Jdazuelos/DRMS; 143 (UP RT), Dream69/DRMS; 143 (LO), Isselee/DRMS; 146-147 (BACKGROUND), Stokkete/DRMS; 148-149 (BACKGROUND), World History Archive/TF; 150-151 (LO), IMAGNO/Austrian Archives/TF; 150-151 (BACKGROUND), Reinhold Leitner/SS; 152 (UP), Glenn Nagel/DRMS; 152 (CTR), Fabio Formaggio/DRMS; 152 (LO), Ron Chapple/DRMS; 153 (UP), Isselee/DRMS; 153 (LO), Linda Bair/DRMS; 154-155 (UP), Curioustravelers/DRMS; 154 (LO LE), Suriyaphoto/DRMS; 154 (LO RT), Sueburtonphotography/DRMS; 154 (LO CTR), Styve Reineck/SS; 155 (UP RT), Iakov Filimonov/DRMS; 155 (LO LE), Rudra Narayan Mitra/DRMS; 155 (LO RT), Celso Pupo rodrigues/DRMS; 156 (UP), Ericus/DRMS; 156 (LO LE), 3drenderings/DRMS; 156 (LO RT), Svetlana Larina/DRMS; 157 (UP), Olivier Le Queinec/DRMS; 157 (CTR LE), Dieter Hawlan/DRMS; 157 (LO-A), Roman Samokhin/DRMS; 157 (LO-B), Duncan Noakes/DRMS; 157 (LO-C), Dragoneye/DRMS; 157 (LO-D), Iakov Filimonov/DRMS; 157 (CTR RT), The Granger Collection/TF

Answer Key [158–170]

158 (CTR), Iakov Filimonov/DRMS; 158 (LO RT), Kotomiti_okuma/DRMS; 158 (UP), Willyam Bradberry/SS; 158 (LO LE), Sombra12/DRMS; 159 (LO RT), Nicholas Piccillo/DRMS; 159 (UP RT), Nahuel Condino/DRMS; 159 (LO LE), The Asahi Shimbun/GI; 160 (CTR), Greenland/DRMS; 160 (LO), Mattiass/DRMS; 160 (UP), EQRoy/SS; 161 (UP LE), Igor Terekhov/DRMS; 161 (UP RT), Kenneth D Durden/DRMS; 161 (LO), Sarah2/DRMS; 162 (UP), Pavel Losevsky/DRMS; 162 (LO), Vladimir Melnikov/SS; 163 (UP), Steve Byland/DRMS; 164 (UP RT), Mocnypunkt/DRMS; 164 (LO RT), Aliaksei Asipovich/DRMS; 164 (UP LE), Nick Pavlakis/SS; 164 (LO LE), TF; 165 (UP), Andrey Burmakin/DRMS; 165 (LO), Olga Kovalenko/DRMS; 166 (UP), Yvdavyd/DRMS; 167 (UP LE), Maxriesgo/DRMS; 167 (LO), Isselee/DRMS; 167 (UP RT), Corey A. Ford/DRMS; 168 (LO), Jdazuelos/DRMS; 169 (LO LE), Stokkete/DRMS; 169 (LO RT), Suriyaphoto/DRMS; 169 (UP), Isselee/DRMS; 170 (LO), Godfer/DRMS; 170 (UP), Duncan Noakes/DRMS

Copyright © 2015
National Geographic Society

All rights reserved. Reproduction of the whole
or any part of the contents without written
permission from the publisher is prohibited.

**Staff for This Book**
Priyanka Sherman and Amy Briggs,
    *Project Editors*
Julide Dengel, *Associate Art Director*
Kelley Miller and Lori Epstein,
    *Senior Illustrations Editors*
Angela Modany, *Editorial Assistant*
Rachel Kenny, *Design Production Assistant*
Callie Bonnacorsy, *Special Projects Assistant*
Grace Hill, *Managing Editor*
Alix Inchausti, *Production Editor*
Lewis R. Bassford, *Production Manager*
Darrick McRae, *Production Services*
Susan Borke, *Legal and Business Affairs*

**Published by the National Geographic Society**
Gary E. Knell, *President and CEO*
John M. Fahey, *Chairman of the Board*
Melina Gerosa Bellows, *Chief Education Officer*
Declan Moore, *Chief Media Officer*
Hector Sierra, *Senior Vice President and
    General Manager, Book Division*

**Editorial, Design, and Production by
Bender Richardson White**
Lionel Bender, *Editor*
Ben White, *Design*
Sharon Hortensio, *Picture Research*
Kim Richardson, *Production*
Nancy Honovich, Alicia Klepeis, Kathryn Hulick
Gargolinksi, Jack Silbert, Jeri Cipriano, Karina
Hamalainen, *Contributors*

**Senior Management Team, Kids Publishing
and Media** Nancy Laties Feresten, *Senior Vice
President*; Erica Green, *Vice President, Editorial
Director, Kids Books*; Julie Vosburgh Agnone,
*Vice President, Operations*; Jennifer Emmett,
*Vice President, Content*; Michelle Sullivan, *Vice
President, Video and Digital Initiatives*; Eva
Absher-Schantz, *Vice President, Visual Identity*;
Amanda Larsen, *Design Director, Kids Books*;
Rachel Buchholz, *Editor and Vice President,
NG Kids magazine*; Jay Sumner, *Photo Director*;
Hannah August, *Marketing Director*; R. Gary
Colbert, *Production Director*

**Digital** Laura Goertzel, *Manager*; Sara Zeglin,
*Senior Producer*; Bianca Bowman, *Assistant
Producer*; Natalie Jones, *Senior Product
Manager*

The National Geographic Society
is one of the world's largest
nonprofit scientific and
educational organizations.
Founded in 1888 to "increase and
diffuse geographic knowledge," the
Society works to inspire people to care about
the planet. National Geographic reflects the
world through its magazines, television
programs, films, music and radio, books, DVDs,
maps, exhibitions, live events, school
publishing programs, interactive media and
merchandise. *National Geographic* magazine,
the Society's official journal, published in
English and 38 local-language editions, is read
by more than 60 million people each month.
The National Geographic Channel reaches 440
million households in 38 languages in
171 countries. National Geographic Digital
Media receives more than 25 million visitors a
month. National Geographic has funded more
than 10,000 scientific research, conservation
and exploration projects and supports an
education program promoting geography
literacy.

For more information, please visit
nationalgeographic.com, call
1-800-NGS LINE (647-5463), or write
to the following address:

National Geographic Society
1145 17th Street N.W.
Washington, D.C. 20036-4688 U.S.A.

Visit us online at
nationalgeographic.com/books

For librarians and teachers:
ngchildrensbooks.org

More for kids from National Geographic:
kids.nationalgeographic.com

For information about special discounts
for bulk purchases, please contact
National Geographic Books Special Sales:
ngspecsales@ngs.org

For rights or permissions inquiries, please
contact National Geographic Books Subsidiary
Rights: ngbookrights@ngs.org

Paperback ISBN: 978-1-4263-2084-2
Reinforced library binding ISBN:
978-1-4263-2085-9

Printed in the United States of America
15/QGT-CML/1

# Wanna know WHY you're such a QUIZ WHIZ?

Find out what activates that big brain of yours and how it works in this cool book, filled with fun facts, challenges, puzzles, and neuroscience!

## BRAIN GAMES

NATIONAL GEOGRAPHIC KiDS

FEATURING CHALLENGES FROM THE HIT NATIONAL GEOGRAPHIC CHANNEL SHOW "BRAIN GAMES"!

THE MIND-BLOWING SCIENCE OF YOUR AMAZING BRAIN
JENNIFER SWANSON

## CHECK YOUR MEMORY

How much can your brain remember? Put it to the test.

### CHALLENGE

Read this list three times. Then cover it. Now get a pencil and a piece of paper. Write down the words you remember. How many did you get right? Five? Eight? Three? If you are like most people, you may have gotten five to seven of the words. But how did your brain manage to remember any of these words at all?

| CHAIR | RAINBOW | BUTTERFLY |
| CLOCK | COMPUTER | APPLE |
| HOUSE | SCISSORS | GLOBE |
| GUITAR | LIGHTBULB | HAMMER |

### WHAT EXACTLY IS HAPPENING?

Your brain has two types of memory: short-term and long-term. Short-term memory lasts anywhere from 15 to 30 seconds. Sometimes even up to a minute. That's about the time it takes for your computer to restart. Long-term memory is anything you can remember for longer than that.

When you read through the list, one loop of neurons went back and forth from the visual cortex to the frontal cortex. Another loop went from your auditory circuit to the frontal cortex. The hippocampus acts like the middleman. It shuttles information from your short-term memory to your long-term memory and back. In fewer than 15 seconds, a short-term memory was created.

Cover the picture. Now get a pencil and a piece of paper. Write down the pictures you remember. How many did you get right? If you go back and look, you will see that these are pictures of the words in the last challenge. Did you get more of them right this time? Why?

### WHAT EXACTLY IS HAPPENING?

Looking at pictures actually helps your brain to remember better. Short-term memory, also called working memory, relies heavily on the visual cortex. Words that are read are processed very quickly by our brains. They don't stick around for very long. But recording a picture in your brain takes longer. The more time spent looking at the picture, the better the memory. Saying a word out loud does the same thing. It takes longer to speak a word than it does to read it. That is why you remember better when you say it aloud. The lesson? When you are doing last-minute cramming for a test, look at pictures and speak things out loud. You memory—and your test score—will thank you.

YOUR SHORT-TERM MEMORY CAN HOLD ONLY ABOUT SEVEN THINGS AT ONE TIME

NATIONAL GEOGRAPHIC KiDS

AVAILABLE WHEREVER BOOKS ARE SOLD
Get a fun freebie at natgeo.com/kids/funpack

© 2015 National Geographic Society